Jeffery Foust

Bosnia and Herzegovina Travel Guide 2024

Discover Enchanting Landscapes, Cultural Gems, and Unforgettable Experiences Across this Hidden European Gem

Copyright © 2023 Jeffery Foust

All Right Reserved

No part of this publication may be reproduced, distributed, or transmitted in any form or by any means, including photocopying, recording, or other electronic or mechanical methods, without the prior written permission of the author, except in the case of brief quotations embodied in critical reviews and specific other noncommercial uses permitted by copyright law.

This publication is protected by copyright law and international treaties. Unauthorized reproduction or distribution of this publication, or any portion of it, may result in severe civil and criminal penalties and will be prosecuted to the maximum extent possible under the law.

Every effort has been made to ensure that the contents of this publication are accurate and up-to-date. However, the author makes no warranties or representations, express or implied, regarding the information's completeness, accuracy, or reliability.

The views and opinions expressed in this publication are those of the author and do not necessarily reflect any agency or organization's official policy or position.

Table of Contents

Table of Contents 2
Introduction 7
   What Makes Bosnia & Herzegovina Unique 11
   Geography and Climate 14
   Best Time to Visit 16
   Visa Requirements 19
   Currency and Banking 23
   Language and Communication 25
   Getting There 29
      Via Air 29
      Land Routes 33
   Getting Around 37
   Discovering Cities 39
      Sarajevo 39
      Mostar 44
      Banja Luka 50
      Blagaj 55
      Trebinje 59
   Exploring Nature 63
      Plitvice Lakes National Park 63

    Una National Park 66

    Vrelo Bosne 68

    Sutjeska National Park 71

    Kravica Waterfalls 74

Embracing Culture and History 77

Bosnian Traditions 80

Festivals and Events 83

    Sarajevo Film Festival 83

    Mostar Summer Fest 85

Bosnian Arts and Crafts 87

    Handicrafts and Souvenirs 89

Traditional Music and Dance 92

Culinary Adventures 95

    Bosnian Cuisine 95

    Must-Try Dishes 97

    Popular Local Restaurants 100

    Street Food Delights 103

Outdoor Activities 105

    Hiking and Trekking 105

    Rafting on the Neretva River 106

    Skiing in the Bosnian Mountains 109

    Cycling Adventures 111

Entertainment and Nightlife 114

    Live Music Venues 114

Nightclubs and Bar 116
Staying Safe and Healthy 118
  Safety Tips.. 118
  Health Precautions.. 121
  Emergency Information 123
  Local Healthcare Facilities.. 125
Cultural Etiquette... 128
Useful Resources 131
  Helpful Apps.. 131
  Useful Websites 135
Conclusion 138

An Open Letter from the Author

Dear Readers,

I am thrilled to present to you the "*Bosnia and Herzegovina Travel Guide*" your ultimate companion to the captivating landscapes and rich cultural tapestry of this remarkable country. As you flip through the pages of this guide, you are embarking on a journey of exploration, discovery, and unparalleled beauty.

Whether you picked up this guide to facilitate stress-free planning for your upcoming trip to Bosnia and Herzegovina or you're curious to discover if it's the perfect destination for your next vacation, I commend you for taking the first step. You are among the 1% of individuals who opt to savor the finest experiences life has to offer.

Bosnia and Herzegovina are a treasure trove of natural wonders, historical richness, and boundless opportunities for unforgettable experiences. This guide serves as your key to unraveling every facet of this extraordinary country, from its picturesque landscapes and historical sites to the welcoming communities that call Bosnia and Herzegovina home.

I have dedicated considerable effort to compile this guide, ensuring that you have access to the most current, authentic, and comprehensive information. My goal is to equip you with everything you need to make the most of your adventure in this enchanting land.

Warm Regards,

Jeffery Foust

Jeffery Foust,

Travel-Expert

Introduction

Welcome to Bosnia and Herzegovina, a land of rich cultural heritage, stunning landscapes, and warm hospitality. Nestled in the center of Southeast Europe, this captivating country is frequently referred to as the "**heart-shaped land**" owing unique geographical shape. As you embark on your journey through Bosnia and Herzegovina, prepare to be enchanted by its diverse combination of influences from both Eastern and Western civilizations.

The capital city, *Sarajevo*, stands as a testament to this harmonious coexistence, where historic Ottoman architecture gracefully mingles with Austro-Hungarian elegance. Explore the cobblestone streets of Baarija, the old bazaar, where the aroma of traditional Bosnian coffee wafts through the air, inviting you to savor a moment of relaxation. For history enthusiasts, a visit to the Latin Bridge is a must, as it was the site of the assassination of [Archduke Franz Ferdinand](), an event that ignited World War I. The War Tunnel Museum offers a poignant glimpse into the country's recent history, giving insight into the strength of the Bosnian people during the siege of Sarajevo.

The breathtaking vistas that stretch across the nation will enthrall nature enthusiasts. A UNESCO World Heritage Site, Plitvice Lakes National Park is home to a number of gorgeous lakes and waterfalls encircled by lush vegetation, making it a haven for hikers and nature lovers. Apart from that, the Kravica Waterfalls offer a cool haven where guests are welcome to enjoy the area's breathtaking scenery.

Try the savory pastry called Burek, which is filled with spinach, cheese, or meat, and the little grilled sausages called Ćevapi. For a truly authentic dining experience, pair your meal with a glass of rakija, a traditional fruit brandy. The Bosnian people have the most incredible hospitality; they greet guests with wide smiles and sincere warmth that makes a lasting impression.

Get involved with the community, exchange tales, and become fully immersed in Bosnia and Herzegovina's colorful cultural fabric. Bosnia and Herzegovina offer a travel experience that goes beyond the typical, whether you choose to explore historical sites, stroll through quaint villages, or just take in the peace and quiet of the outdoors. Accept the special fusion of culture, history, and scenic beauty that makes this amazing place what it is.

Welcome to Bosnia and Herzegovina, and a journey unlike any other.

Get your FREE book

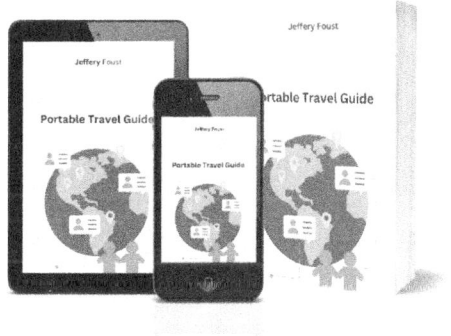

Please visit https://tinyurl.com/travel-with-jeffery for additional resources and to engage with my newsletter.

I also want to reward you for purchasing my book. To get the reward which is a travel planner; kindly click on this link below or open the link on your browser.

https://tinyurl.com/travel_with-jeffery

I hope you love the travel planner!

What Makes Bosnia & Herzegovina Unique

One of the defining traits of Bosnia and Herzegovina is its impressive historical heritage. The country has been a crossroads of civilizations for centuries, with influences from the Ottoman Empire, Austro-Hungarian Empire, and the Byzantine and Roman eras obvious in its architecture, cuisine, and traditions.

The iconic Stari Most bridge in Mostar, a UNESCO World Heritage site, is a testament to the Ottoman legacy, while the diverse religious landmarks, comprising mosques, churches, and synagogues, showcase the country's religious tolerance. Nature plays a pivotal role in the peculiarity of Bosnia and Herzegovina. The country is adorned with picturesque landscapes, from the lush greenery of the Una National Park to the serene waters of the Buna River.

The Dinaric Alps paint a dramatic backdrop, giving a haven for outdoor enthusiasts with activities such as hiking, rafting, and skiing. The Plitvice Lakes, a sequence of cascading waterfalls and crystal-clear lakes, add to the country's natural allure, generating it a haven for eco-tourism.

The distinctive character of Bosnia is largely shaped by the kindness and tenacity of its people. Even with a convoluted and conflict-filled past, the people here have an open and genuine attitude toward life. Whether sipping traditional Bosnian coffee in Sarajevo's Baščaršija district or striking up a heartfelt conversation with locals who are eager to share their stories, visitors will be completely engulfed in the warmth of Bosnian hospitality. Another aspect of Bosnia and Herzegovina's distinctiveness is its food scene.

The delicious food of the nation, which includes items like cevapi (grilled minced meat), burek (pastry filled with meat, cheese, or vegetables), and baklava, reflects the varied cultural influences that have shaped the nation. Every taste narrates the history of the country and the blending of diverse culinary customs. Bosnia and Herzegovina are known for its natural and cultural wonders, but it's also incredibly peaceful. This hidden gem, located away from the bustle of more popular tourist spots, lets visitors explore at their own leisure and find hidden treasures like the quaint village of Počitelj or the medieval town of Jajce.

When you travel through Bosnia and Herzegovina, you'll discover that the true warmth of its people sits alongside its stunning scenery and historical landmarks, making it a truly unique place. It is a location where the past and present come together to create a truly unique experience.

Geography and Climate

The Dinaric Alps stretch across the western and southern sections of the country, offering breathtaking panoramas and excellent chances for hiking and skiing. The highest peak, Magli, stands proudly at 2,386 meters (7,828 feet) above sea level, providing not merely a challenging ascent but also unparalleled views of the surrounding landscapes.

In contrast, the northern and central regions boast fertile plains and river valleys, particularly along the Sava and Neretva rivers. These areas are dotted with charming towns and villages, each with its distinctive character and a warm welcome for visitors. The country's capital, Sarajevo, is situated in a valley and serves as a vibrant cultural and historic hub. Bosnia & Herzegovina experiences a varied climate, with a blend of Mediterranean and Continental influences.

Summers are broadly warm and dry, generating it an ideal time to explore the outdoor treasures the country has to offer. Average temperatures range from 20°C to 30°C (68F to 86F) during this season.

The arrival of winter turns the land into a wintry paradise, particularly in the highland areas with copious amounts of snowfall. From December through February, skiers flock to the well-equipped resorts tucked away in the Dinaric Alps. For those who intend to travel during this wonderful season, it is imperative to pack appropriate cold-weather gear because winter temperatures can drop below freezing.

Because of their moderate temperatures, spring and fall are ideal for taking in the natural beauty and cultural treasures without having to deal with extreme weather.

Furthermore, late spring and early autumn are the best seasons to visit if you're looking for a balance between nice weather and less visitors. I will elaborate more on this in the next few pages.

Best Time to Visit

The country offers a diverse scope of attractions and activities throughout the year, so the best time to visit relies on your preferences and interests.

Spring (April to June): Spring is a wonderful time to explore Bosnia and Herzegovina. The weather during this period is mild and pleasant, with blooming landscapes and vibrant greenery.

This is an ideal time for nature enthusiasts and outdoor activities. You can enjoy hiking in the beautiful national parks, such as Una National Park, or take a leisurely stroll through the charming streets of cities like Sarajevo and Mostar.

Summer (July to August): Summer is the peak visitor season in Bosnia and Herzegovina. The weather is warm, and the days are long, permitting for extended exploration.

This is the perfect time for cultural experiences, as numerous festivals and events take place during the summer months. You can attend the Sarajevo Film Festival or explore the historical sites, like the Old Bridge in Mostar, under clear skies. Keep in mind that well-known destinations might be crowded during this time.

Autumn (September to November): Bosnia and Herzegovina have a special charm during the fall. The landscapes change to a breathtaking display of fall colors, producing a charming scene. This is a great time of year for outdoor activities because the weather is still pleasant. Since autumn is also harvest season, you can go to traditional festivals and savor delectable local cuisine. There is less of a crowd and a calmer environment for exploring.

Winter (December to February): If you like winter sports, especially, Bosnia and Herzegovina's winters are truly magical.

You can enjoy the excitement of skiing or snowboarding at some of the nation's top ski resorts, like Jahorina and Bjelasnica. The festive lights that adorn the cities create a warm and joyous ambiance.

Winter is the ideal season to visit if you enjoy winter sports or want to take in the beauty of snow-covered scenery. Because Bosnia and Herzegovina have a continental climate, you should think about how tolerant you are to various types of weather. While winters, particularly in mountainous areas, can be frigid and snowy, summers can also be warm.

Look for festivals and events that suit your interests on the local calendar. These can offer special perspectives on the region's rich cultural diversity. If you'd rather have a more sedate experience, think about going in the shoulder seasons of spring or autumn, when fewer people are there. The ideal time to travel to Bosnia and Herzegovina ultimately depends on you.

Visa Requirements

Your nationality determines whether you require a visa to visit Bosnia and Herzegovina. Most countries' citizens can visit Bosnia and Herzegovina without a visa for up to 90 days within a 180-day period. There are, however, a few exceptions.

Citizens of the following countries do not need a visa to visit Bosnia and Herzegovina:

All European Union member states	
Andorra	Liechtenstein
Argentina	Mexico
Australia	Montenegro
Brazil	New Zealand
Canada	Nicaragua
Chile	North Macedonia

Costa Rica	Norway
Cuba	Serbia
Ecuador	Panama
El Salvador	Paraguay
Guatemala	Peru
Honduras	San Marino
Iceland	Singapore
Israel	South Korea
Japan	Switzerland
Taiwan	Turkey
United States	United Kingdom
Uruguay	Venezuela

Visa Types:

Essentially, there are two types of visas you can obtain for your trip to Bosnia. Below, we outline the visa options and how they work:

• **Short-stay visa (C):** Allows stays of up to 90 days within a period of 180 days for tourist, business, or family visits.

• **Long-stay visa (D):** For persons pursuing employment, education, or other objectives that last longer than 90 days.

The Visa Application Procedure:

a. Complete the online application form (https://www.visahq.com/bosnia-herzegovina/)

b. Gather the following documents:

1. A valid passport with at least three months validity beyond your scheduled departure date is required.
2. Two passport-sized photographs.
3. Proof of travel and accommodation.
4. Evidence of sufficient financial resources.
5. Travel insurance.
6. Receipt for Visa fee paid.
7. Make an appointment with the Bosnia and Herzegovina embassy or consulate in your area.

8. Submit your application and show up for the interview.
9.

Time Required for Processing:

Visa processing takes at least 15 days and, in rare situations, up to 30 days. Apply early, especially during high seasons.

Further information:

- If you are staying in a private residence for more than three days, you must register with the local police within 24 hours of arrival.
- Keep your passport on you at all times as identification.
- Airlines may refuse boarding to passengers arriving on a one-way ticket or exceeding a three-month return date.
- When visiting religious sites, observe local norms and dress modestly.

Currency and Banking

The official currency of Bosnia and Herzegovina is the Convertible Mark (BAM), abbreviated as KM. Introduced in 1995, the Convertible Mark replaced the Yugoslav Dinar, and its stable value has contributed to the economic growth of the country. The Convertible Mark is divided into 100 fenings, and you'll frequently find coins in denominations of 1, 2, and 5 KM, as well as banknotes in 10, 20, 50, 100, and 200 KM. Bosnia and Herzegovina boast a well-established banking infrastructure, making it convenient for travelers to access financial services.

Major cities and well-known tourist destinations are equipped with a network of banks, ATMs, and currency exchange offices. ATMs are commonly available, adopting major credit and debit cards. Look for ATMs affiliated with international networks such as Visa and Mastercard for hassle-free transactions. It's advisable to inform your bank about your travel plans to avoid any potential challenges with card usage abroad.

Despite the widespread availability of ATMs, it makes sense to keep some local currency on hand, particularly in more rural areas. Airports, tourist destinations, and urban areas are frequently home to currency exchange offices. To get the best deal, it's advised to compare exchange rates and fees. Larger establishments such as restaurants and hotels generally accept credit cards. But it's a good idea to have some cash on hand, particularly if you're visiting markets or smaller establishments where there might not be much card acceptance.

In Bosnia and Herzegovina, banking hours usually correspond with regular European schedules. With variable hours, banks are open Monday through Friday; they are closed on weekends and public holidays. Conversely, ATMs offer cash access around-the-clock. To avoid any unforeseen problems with your cards, let your bank know about your travel schedule and destination.

As a backup in case of unforeseen events, think about keeping a small amount of emergency cash in a safe place. Accept the customs of the place by reserving your cards for larger purchases and using cash for smaller ones. To prevent confusion during transactions, familiarize yourself with the appearance of local coins and banknotes. You can ensure a seamless and pleasurable travel experience by becoming acquainted with Bosnia and Herzegovina's currency and banking system.

Language and Communication

Bosnia and Herzegovina are a multilingual country with three official languages: *Bosnian, Croatian*, and *Serbian*. These languages are mutually intelligible, and locals often adopt the term "BCS" to collectively refer to them. While this linguistic diversity may appear complex, it reflects the historic and cultural nuances of the region. Bosnian, written in both Latin and Cyrillic scripts, serves as one of the official languages. It is primarily spoken by Bosniaks, the largest ethnic group in the country.

Visitors will find that numerous road signs, official documents, and public announcements are in Bosnian. Croatian, another official language, shares linguistic similarities with Bosnian and Serbian. It is spoken primarily by Croats, particularly in areas bordering Croatia. The utilization of the Latin alphabet distinguishes Croatian from the other two languages, adding a distinctive touch to the country's linguistic landscape.

Serbian, the third official language, is spoken mainly by the Serb population. Like Bosnian, it is written in both Latin and Cyrillic scripts.

Though there are minor variances that represent the cultural differences within Bosnia and Herzegovina, speakers of Serbian will find a certain familiarity with the language. Regional dialects may also be spoken, particularly in more isolated areas, in addition to the official tongues. The historical contacts with neighboring countries have left a lasting impression on these dialects. Locals value it when visitors speak with them in their own tongues because it gives your trip a more intimate feel.

As a tourist, understanding and embracing local greetings and courtesy phrases will not only open doors but also hearts.

1. **Basic Greetings:**

    Dobar dan (DOH-bar dahn): Good day.

    Dobro jutro (DOH-bro YOO-tro): Good morning.

    Dobra veer (DOH-bra VEH-cher): Good evening.

    Laku no (LAH-koo nohch): Good night.

2. **Common Courtesies:**

    Molim (MOH-leem): Please.

    Hvala (HVAH-lah): Thank you.

    Molim vas (MOH-leem vahs): Please (formal).

    Hvala vam (HVAH-lah vahm): Thank you (formal).

    Izvinite (IZ-vee-nee-teh): Excuse me/sorry.

    Oprostite (O-pro-sti-teh): I'm sorry (more formal)

3. **Traditional Bosnian Phrases:**

    Selam aleikum (SEH-lahm ah-lei-kum): Traditional Islamic greeting, meaning "Peace be upon you."

    Bog (BOHG): God (common in expressions, like "Bog s tobom" - God be with you).

    Zdravo (ZDRAH-vo): Hello.

4. **Social Niceties:**

    Kako ste? (KAH-ko steh): How are you?

    Dobro sam, hvala (DOH-bro sahm, HVAH-lah): I'm fine, thank you.

    Drago mi je (DRAH-go mee yeh): Nice to meet you.

5. **Saying Goodbye**:

Dovienja (doh-vee-JEH-nyah): Goodbye.

Zbogom (ZBOH-gohm): Farewell.

Ciao (CHOW): Used informally, like saying "bye."

Never forget that Bosnians value sincerity and real relationships. It is not uncommon for locals to extend their greetings and show concern for your welfare. You are more than just a visitor to this amazing country; please feel free to return the favor with warmth and an open heart.

Getting There

Depending on your budget and time limits, there are several ways to get to Bosnia & Herzegovina.

Via Air

Bosnia and Herzegovina have two international airports, Sarajevo International Airport (SJJ) and Tuzla International Airport (TZL), which serve as gateways to this fascinating country.

Sarajevo International Airport (SJJ), the larger of the two, is about 12 kilometers from the capital city of Sarajevo. It serves as a hub for several airlines, including Turkish Airlines, Austrian Airlines, Lufthansa, Lufthansa, Ryanair, Wizz Air, Pegasus, Air Serbia, and Croatia Airlines, providing direct flights to major European cities and beyond.

Tuzla International Airport (TZL), located in Bosnia and Herzegovina's northeastern region, acts as a regional hub, mostly serving domestic and low-cost carriers. It has direct flights to a number of European cities, including Vienna, Bratislava, Budapest, and Memmingen.

Planning Your Trip

Careful planning is required before going on your air excursion to Bosnia and Herzegovina to ensure a seamless and comfortable travel experience. Here's a detailed guide to air travel planning:

1. **Select an Airport for Departure**: Sarajevo International Airport (SJJ) and Tuzla International Airport (TZL) are the two international airports in Bosnia and Herzegovina. Sarajevo International Airport is the larger and more centrally located of the two, serving as the country's principal gateway. Tuzla International Airport, located in the northeastern region, serves visitors visiting nearby cities.

2. **Choose Your Airline**: Numerous airlines fly to Bosnia and Herzegovina from major cities in Europe, North America, and the Middle East, with direct and connecting flights. Among the well-known airlines are:

    • **Turkish Airlines:** Direct flights from Istanbul and connecting flights from various European cities are available.

- **Austrian Airlines**: Offers direct flights from Vienna as well as connecting flights from a number of European cities.

- **Lufthansa**: Direct flights from Frankfurt and Munich, as well as connecting flights from other European locations.

- **Ryanair:** Provides low-cost flights to Bosnia and Herzegovina from numerous European cities.

- **Wizz Air**: Offers low-cost flights from numerous European destinations to Sarajevo International Airport.

- **Pegasus Airlines**: This airline has direct flights from Istanbul as well as connecting flights from other Turkish cities.

- **Air Serbia**: Direct flights from Belgrade and connecting flights from other Balkan cities are available.

- **Croatia Airlines**: Offers direct flights from Zagreb as well as connections from other Croatian cities.

3. **Book Your Flight Tickets**: Once you've decided on an airline and a departure airport, it's time to purchase your plane tickets. Flight schedules and ticket sales are normally released many months in advance. When you

book your tickets early, you might get the best rates, especially during peak travel seasons. Consider using online travel services or contacting airlines directly to compare prices and discover the best fares.

4. **Check Visa Requirements**: You may need a visa to enter Bosnia and Herzegovina, depending on your nationality. Visa requirements differ depending on the length of your stay and your country of origin.

5. **Prepare Travel Documents**: Gather all essential travel documents, including your passport, visa (if applicable), travel insurance, and any additional important documentation. Throughout your journey, keep these documents arranged and easily accessible.

6. **Check-In and Boarding processes**: Learn the check-in and boarding processes for your preferred airline. Online check-in is usually available 24 hours before departure, allowing you to save time at the airport. Arrive at the airport at least two hours before your scheduled departure time to allow for check-in, security screening, and boarding procedures.

7. **Baggage Allowance and Fees**: To avoid any surprises, carefully check your airline's baggage allowance and fee rules. Learn about the weight and size restrictions for carry-on and checked baggage. If you exceed your allowance, you may be charged additional fees.

8. **In-Flight Amenities and Services**: To enhance your travel experience, most airlines provide a variety of in-flight amenities and services. In-flight meals, snacks, beverages, entertainment systems, and Wi-Fi connectivity are examples. Check with your preferred airline to find out what facilities and services are available on your flight.

Land Routes

While flight is the most convenient way to go to Bosnia and Herzegovina, there are various other choices for getting there by land.

Bosnia and Herzegovina have 11 border crossings with neighboring nations. Tourists' most popular border crossings are:

Croatia:

   1. Neum-Klecak (Road)
   2. Kardclj-Ivanić Grad (Road)

3. Brčko-Gunja (Road and Rail)
4. Metković-Šurmanci (Road)

Serbia:

5. Bijeljina-Batković (Road and Rail)
6. Zvornik-Mali Zvornik (Road and Rail)
7. Srebrenica-Ljubovija (Road)
8. Rudo-Scepan Polje (Road)

Montenegro:

9. Gornji Brčak-Cipci (Road)
10. Metaljka-Hum (Road)
11. Bileća-Gruda (Road)
12. Klobuk-Ubli (Road)

North Macedonia:

13. Vrbnica-Vrbno (Road)

A valid passport is required to enter Bosnia & Herzegovina via land. Most Western European countries, the United States, Canada, Australia, and New Zealand citizens do not require a visa to enter Bosnia and Herzegovina for up to 90 days. Citizens of other countries should check with their local Bosnian embassy or consulate to discover if they need a visa.

You may be requested to present documentation of onward travel as well as sufficient finances for your stay, in addition to your passport. It is also advisable to bring some Bosnian cash with you, as not all shops in Bosnia and Herzegovina take foreign currencies.

Bosnia and Herzegovina's border crossing procedures are generally simple. You will be required to show your passport to the immigration officer and may be questioned about your travel. You may be requested to open your luggage for inspection as well.

Get your FREE book

Please visit https://tinyurl.com/travel-with-jeffery for additional resources and to engage with my newsletter.

I also want to reward you for purchasing my book. To get the reward which is a travel planner; kindly click on this link below or open the link on your browser.

https://tinyurl.com/travel-with-jeffery

I hope you love the travel planner!

Getting Around

Getting around Bosnia and Herzegovina is simple and inexpensive. Buses, trains, autos, and taxis are among the numerous modes of transportation.

In Bosnia and Herzegovina, buses are the most frequent kind of transportation. There is a comprehensive bus network that connects all of the major cities and communities. Buses are another viable alternative for reaching out to smaller villages and rural areas.

Bus travel is typically inexpensive and comfortable. Buses are often air-conditioned and contemporary. They also include luggage compartments where you may store your items.

Bus tickets can be purchased at bus stops or directly from the bus driver. Tickets can also be purchased in advance online.

Trains are a slower but more picturesque mode of transportation in Bosnia and Herzegovina. The major cities are linked by a number of train routes. The train network, however, is not as large as the bus network.

In general, train travel is more expensive than bus travel. Trains, on the other hand, are frequently more pleasant and offer greater legroom.

Train tickets are available at train stations and online.

Travelers who want to see Bosnia and Herzegovina at their own leisure can consider renting a car. Car rental companies can be found in all major cities.

Driving is typically safe and simple in Bosnia & Herzegovina. You should be aware, however, that some roads are in bad condition. You should also expect to drive over high terrain.

Taxis are a convenient mode of transportation in Bosnia and Herzegovina. Taxis are easily accessible in all major cities and towns.

Taxis are relatively inexpensive. You should, however, always settle on a price with the taxi driver before getting in.

Discovering Cities

Sarajevo

Sarajevo, the capital of Bosnia and Herzegovina, is rich in historical attractions that reflect its diverse cultural and historical heritage. Located in the heart of the Balkans, Sarajevo played a central role in shaping the region and its history. As you wander through this fascinating city, you'll encounter architectural marvels, vivid reminders of the past, and vibrant cultural centers.

One of the most iconic landmarks is the Latin Bridge, forever etched in history as the site of the assassination of Archduke Franz Ferdinand in 1914, the event that sparked the First World War. Walking across this elegant Ottoman-era bridge, you can does not simply feel the weight of historical significance. Located in the heart of the Ottoman Old Town, Bascarsija Square is a lively market that dates back to the 15th century. This labyrinthine bazaar is a testament to Sarajevo's diversity and culture, where you can immerse yourself in the sights and sounds of traditional crafts, local delicacies and the warm hospitality of the Bosnian people.

The Sarajevo skyline is graced by the enchanting Sebilj Fountain, an ornate wooden fountain in the center of Bascarsija Square. Built in the 18th century, it is a symbol of life and vitality, attracting locals and tourists who gather around its clean waters.

While walking the cobblestone streets, don't miss the Gazi Husrev-beg Mosque, an architectural gem from the Ottoman era. With its intricate design and peaceful surroundings, it is a spiritual and historical paradise. Next to the mosque you will find Gazi Husrev-beg Bezistan, a covered market where merchants have been selling their goods for centuries. Head up into the mountains surrounding Sarajevo and you'll find the Yellow Citadel with panoramic views of the city below.

This medieval fortress is a silent testament to Sarajevo and resilience through the ages. Get a moving reminder of recent history at the War Tunnel Museum in Sarajevo. Built during the Bosnian war, this underground passage was a lifeline for the city and its inhabitants.

The museum offers a moving experience, documenting the determination of the people of Sarajevo in difficult times. End your historical journey at the Eternal Flame Memorial, dedicated to the people and fighters who fell in the War of

Independence. Located in the heart of Sarajevo, this symbol of memory and resilience embodies the spirit and resilience of the city. Sarajevo's historical landmarks weave together a story of triumphs and challenges, reflecting the enduring soul of this fascinating city.

Bascarsija: This Ottoman-era bazaar is a maze of cobbled streets, bustling markets and traditional Bosnian crafts. Enjoy the smell of freshly brewed coffee as you stroll through the labyrinthine alleys, explore handmade copperware, intricately designed rugs and bask in the warmth of local hospitality.

Sebilj Fountain: Located in the center of Bascarsija, the Sebilj Fountain is an iconic symbol of Sarajevo. Built in the 18th century, this ornate wooden fountain served as a community water source during the Ottoman era. Today it is a charming reminder of the history and history of the city and a popular meeting place for locals and tourists.

Gazi Husrev-beg Mosque: Gazi Husrev-beg Mosque is one of the best examples of Ottoman architecture in the Balkans. Built in the 16th century, the mosque displays intricate geometric patterns and calligraphy. An adjacent courtyard with a fountain and historic bell tower offers a peaceful escape from the hustle and bustle of the city.

Sarajevo City Hall (Vijecnica): A symbol of resilience, Sarajevo City Hall has seen the city both triumph and hardship. Originally built in the Austro-Hungarian style, the grand building was heavily damaged during the Bosnian War, but has been carefully restored. Today, it houses the national and university libraries, a testament to the city's commitment to preserving cultural heritage.

Latin Bridge: History buffs will love walking across the Latin Bridge, infamous for the 1914 assassination of Archduke Franz Ferdinand, which sparked World War I. The bridge offers a charming view of the Miljacka River and the surrounding architecture. it's a painful yet beautiful stop on your cultural journey.

War Childhood Museum: Delve into Sarajevo's more recent history at the War Childhood Museum. This unique institution collects and shares the personal stories and belongings of children who survived the Bosnian war. The exhibits offer a moving and insightful perspective on the impact of conflict on the city and its youngest residents.

National Museum of Bosnia and Herzegovina: The National Museum is a must-see if you want to learn about the region and its cultural and natural heritage. Its exhibits include archaeology, ethnology and natural history, offering a deep dive into the diversity of Bosnia and Herzegovina past and present.

Caffe de Alma: End your cultural tour at Caffe de Alma, a trendy cafe located in the heart of the city. It's not just a coffee break; it's an opportunity to taste Bosnian coffee, chat with locals and enjoy the eclectic atmosphere of modern Sarajevo. In Sarajevo, every corner tells a story and every landmark is a testament to the resilience, diversity and enduring cultural spirit of the city. By exploring these cultural sites, you will undoubtedly discover the unique charm that sets Sarajevo apart as a truly exceptional destination.

Mostar

Standing tall above the Neretva River, the Stari Most Bridge in Mostar is more than just a mere passageway. It serves as a powerful symbol of strength, togetherness, and the unwavering spirit of a city that has withstood the tests of time. This famous bridge, rich with history, represents the beautiful fusion of different cultures that make up the identity of Bosnia and Herzegovina. The Stari Most, also known as the "*Old Bridge*," was constructed in the 16th century under the Ottoman rule and was considered a remarkable feat of engineering during that era.

Suleiman the Magnificent commissioned the bridge to serve as a crucial connection between the Christian and Muslim communities on both sides of Mostar, enhancing the coexistence of these communities in the charming town. The Stari Most's architectural beauty is truly a sight to behold. The bridge is made from local stone and showcases the exceptional workmanship of the Ottoman period. The hump-backed design, seen in many Ottoman bridges, not only enhances its beauty but also provides stability against the strong currents of the Neretva River.

Unfortunately, the Stari Most suffered destruction during the conflicts of the 1990s. In 1993, the bridge fell victim to the destruction of war and crumbled into the river. Nonetheless, the people of Mostar were determined to keep their symbol of unity alive and not let it fade into the past. The Stari Most was reconstructed with extraordinary care, using the original techniques and materials, and reopened in 2004 amid great celebration. As you walk along the Stari Most, you'll be met with stunning views of the Neretva River and the delightful old town that encircles it. Vibrant markets, charming cafes, and historic buildings line the streets, each one telling stories of the past centuries.

For an authentic experience, you should definitely check out the Stari Most during the yearly traditional diving contest. The fearless locals demonstrate their courage by jumping off the bridge and into the cold waters below, a tradition that has been upheld since the bridge was first built.

The cobblestone streets of the Old Bazaar transport you back in time, with the echoes of past generations lingering in the air as you wander through. The architectural style of Mostar reflects a harmonious combination of Ottoman and Austro-Hungarian elements, serving as a visual narrative of the city's rich cultural heritage. The graceful arch of the iconic Stari Most bridge stands as a symbol of the city's resilience and the lasting wounds of its turbulent past. As you wander through the twisting alleys of the Old Bazaar, you'll be surrounded by countless sights, sounds, and smells to take in.

The market stalls are filled with vibrant textiles, handcrafted pottery, and intricate metalwork that display the skilled craftsmanship that has been passed down through the ages. Artisans, most of whom come from generations of family craftsmen, find great satisfaction in their work, producing a genuine and captivating atmosphere. If you're willing to explore the culinary offerings of the Old Bazaar, you'll find treasures like Ćevapi, a grilled minced meat dish, and burek, a savory pastry filled with meat or cheese, just waiting to be tasted.

The Old Bazaar is more than just a collection of tangible treasures - it is a living museum filled with stories.

The people who live here have a genuine warmth that embodies the hospitality of this area. They share stories that bring the ancient buildings and worn-out facades to life. Visitors are welcomed to connect with the historic spirit of Mostar, as conversations echo tales of resilience, unity, and indomitable spirit.

The Old Bazaar is more than just a market - it is a vibrant and essential part of Mostar, embodying its spirit and vitality. It invites explorers to fully embrace its historic streets, to sense the rhythm of the past beneath their steps, and to indulge in the tastes of a resilient culture.

If you ever visit Mostar, make sure to explore the Old Bazaar as it will transport you back in time and immerse you in the rich cultural heritage of Bosnia and Herzegovina. Underneath the imposing presence of Stari Most, within the lively and bustling market, lies more than just a place to visit but a vivid story woven into the essence of Mostar's identity.

The clear waters of the Neretva River make it a perfect spot for diving enthusiasts. The club welcomes divers of all experience levels, making it possible for everyone to explore the incredible sights beneath the water's surface. The underwater scenery is varied, with submerged rock formations, underwater caves, and a variety of aquatic life that will mesmerize you.

At Neretva Diving Club, their committed and welcoming team places safety as a top priority while ensuring the excitement of exploration is not overlooked. Comprehensive diving courses are available for beginners, providing them with essential skills and knowledge to confidently explore the underwater world. Experienced divers can take advantage of the club's special opportunities to explore advanced diving sites and uncover the secrets of the Neretva's underwater world.

The Neretva Diving Club stands out for its dedication to preserving the environment. The club regularly hosts clean-up events to encourage its members to take responsibility for the environment and feel connected to it. The club's infrastructure is created to improve the overall experience. Once divers have finished their thrilling dive, they can unwind at the club's beautiful waterfront facilities, taking in the stunning views of the Neretva River and the surrounding scenery.

In addition, the club hosts social gatherings to foster a strong bond among divers who are united by their love for exploration. Aside from its diving services, the Neretva Diving Club partners with local businesses to offer a well-rounded travel experience.

If you are seeking comfortable lodging, authentic Bosnian food, or outdoor adventures, the club's connections guarantee that your stay in Mostar will be full of excitement and cultural immersion. Neretva Diving Club in

Mostar offers more than just an opportunity to dive; it provides an immersive experience that allows visitors to engage with the natural beauty and cultural richness of Bosnia and Herzegovina. If you're new to diving and looking for adventure, or if you're an experienced diver seeking unexplored waters, this club welcomes you to explore the amazing underwater world of Mostar and create unforgettable memories.

Banja Luka

The Kastel Fortress, located in the heart of Banja Luka, is a timeless symbol of Bosnia and Herzegovina's rich history and cultural heritage. For centuries, the iconic landmark has stood proudly on the left bank of the Vrbas River, observing triumphs, struggles, and the passage of time. The Kastel Fortress, also referred to as Banjalučka tvrđava, has a long history that dates back to the Roman era when it was first built as a military outpost. Over time, it has gone through countless changes, with each new iteration contributing to its distinctive personality.

The Kastel Fortress is strategically positioned to provide both a stunning panoramic view of Banja Luka and a unique insight into the fusion of cultures that have influenced this region. Throughout history, the fortress has fulfilled different roles, evolving from a military stronghold to a cultural center, demonstrating its adaptability as a symbol of resilience. When you visit Kastel Fortress, one of the standout features is the imposing Clock Tower that commands attention against the backdrop of the skyline. Constructed in the Ottoman era, this architectural marvel not only functions as a clock but also reverberates with the tales of bygone times.

When you climb to the top, you will be rewarded with a stunning view of the surrounding landscapes, giving you a special view of the modernity of Banja Luka alongside the ancient charm of the fortress. Not only has the fortress stood the test of time, but it has also evolved into a center for cultural events, concerts, and exhibitions. The well-maintained areas are now home to museums and galleries that display the art, history, and traditions of Bosnia and Herzegovina.

Walking through these exhibits is like taking a journey through the pages of an enthralling novel, with Kastel Fortress acting as the unspoken storyteller. If you love history, are a fan of architecture, or simply enjoy exploring new places, Kastel Fortress in Banja Luka offers an enriching adventure for all.

Each year, the International Theatre Festival is a standout event on Banja Luka's cultural calendar. Talented actors and directors from all over the world come together for this event, presenting a wide variety of theatrical performances that enthrall audiences with their innovation and depth of emotion. The festival is a celebration of theater art and also provides a platform for cultural exchange, promoting a deeper understanding between artists and spectators. If you're a music lover, you'll be delighted to know that Banja Luka is home to the Banski Dvor Cultural Center, which hosts a multitude of musical events all year round. The annual Banja Luka Rock City festival is known for its impressive lineup of rock bands, attracting large crowds and infusing the city with a vibrant and energetic atmosphere. The abundance of galleries spread throughout Banja Luka will captivate art enthusiasts.

The city shows its dedication to promoting local talent through events such as the Banja Luka Art Fair, which provides emerging artists with the chance to showcase their work and engage with a larger audience. Cultural activities in Banja Luka go beyond traditional arts and also include film events. The Banja Luka International Animated Film Festival celebrates the imaginative work of animators worldwide, offering a stage to honor this distinct art form. For a more in-depth exploration of the region's historical and cultural heritage, visitors have the opportunity to discover the Banja Luka City Museum.

The institution is not just a place for artifacts and exhibits about the city's history, but it also holds lectures and events that shed light on Banja Luka's cultural importance in the wider context of Bosnia and Herzegovina. Apart from the planned events, the streets of Banja Luka are filled with spontaneous cultural displays that liven up the atmosphere. Frequent local cafes and bars showcase live music performances, offering visitors a cozy environment to experience the genuine sounds of the area. Experience the diverse culture of Banja Luka, where traditional and contemporary elements come together seamlessly.

Mladen Stojanović Park is a true treasure of Banja Luka, it is a must-see. With over 100 acres of land, this vast green sanctuary beckons visitors to surround themselves with luxuriant gardens, peaceful ponds, and meandering trails. The park's varied plant life, which includes native trees and colorful flowers, provides a beautiful setting for relaxed walks and enjoyable family picnics. The Mladen Stojanović Park is more than just a patch of greenery; it's a haven where residents come together to unwind, engage in sports, and attend cultural gatherings.

If you're looking for a more dynamic experience, Krajina Square is the place to be for recreational activities. The busy square turns into a lively area where locals come together to play sports such as basketball, volleyball, and traditional games native to the region. The energetic vibe is contagious, attracting both fans and onlookers alike. The

Banj Brdo Forest Park is a vast wooded area on the edge of the city, offering a peaceful escape for nature lovers. The park is a haven for hikers and cyclists, with scenic trails meandering through dense forests and offering stunning views of the Vrbas River valley. The historic mosque is surrounded by exquisite landscaping, creating a serene atmosphere that allows visitors to relax and contemplate in a unique setting. The park acts as a link between the past and present, showcasing the city's dedication to preserving its cultural heritage.

Furthermore, Banja Luka has an energetic cultural scene that frequently extends into its parks, in addition to its green spaces. Open-air concerts and art exhibitions transform these leisure spaces into vibrant cultural hubs, where communities come together to celebrate and enjoy the arts.

Blagaj

Blagaj Tekke, situated in the charming village of Blagaj, Bosnia and Herzegovina, is a secret treasure that effortlessly combines history, spirituality, and the beauty of nature. When you start your exploration of this captivating area, it is essential to visit the Blagaj Tekke, which provides a special combination of cultural significance and peacefulness. The Dervish monastery, also known as the tekke, is situated at the foot of a majestic cliff, with the Buna River flowing gracefully below it. The breathtaking setting enhances the otherworldly nature of the spiritual enlightenment it offers.

As you draw near, the peaceful sounds of the river and the gentle rustling of the leaves combine to create a tranquil atmosphere, laying the foundation for a deep connection with the natural world and its history. Built in the Ottoman era, the Blagaj Tekke has endured the passing of time and experienced the changes of many centuries of culture.

The architectural wonder displays a beautiful combination of Ottoman and Mediterranean styles, decorated with detailed carvings and geometric designs. Upon entering, guests are welcomed by a feeling of calm and serenity. The timeless spirituality of the central prayer hall is enhanced by the traditional Bosnian carpets and Ottoman-era calligraphy that adorn it. The tekke is still a functioning Sufi monastery, offering insight into the timeless spiritual practices that have been passed down through the generations. The Buna River is of great importance, as it originates from a stunning karstic spring that is only a short distance from the tekke.

The clear waters of the river mirror the cliffs and greenery, forming a picture-perfect view. Sipping traditional Bosnian coffee at the riverside cafes provides a fantastic opportunity to admire the stunning views. If you want to fully immerse yourself in the culture, you should definitely plan to attend the yearly dervish ceremonies. During these ceremonies, Sufi practitioners perform captivating rituals that involve music, dance, and chanting. It's an experience like no other. Blagaj Tekke stands as a symbol of the diverse cultural heritage of Bosnia and Herzegovina.

The blend of history, spirituality, and natural wonders makes for an unforgettable journey for travelers looking to forge a deeper connection with the heart and soul of this mesmerizing region. As you meander through the winding streets of Blagaj and experience the friendly welcome of its residents, allow the Blagaj Tekke to be a focal point of your

Bosnian adventure, encouraging you to contemplate the enduring charm of this concealed gem.

Buna Spring is a breathtaking karst spring that showcases the emergence of the Buna River from a cavern, forming a mesmerizing pool of clear turquoise water. Nestled at the foot of a striking cliff, the spring is overlooked by the historic Blagaj Tekke, a Dervish monastery with roots dating back to the 16th century. As Buna Spring comes into view, the imposing cliff and the Dervish monastery perched on top immediately capture your attention, almost as if they are keeping a watchful eye over the peaceful waters below. The bubbling spring's sound is joined by the gentle rustle of leaves, forming a natural symphony that brings instant solace to the soul. One can wander around Buna Spring and enjoy a leisurely walk along the riverbank, passing by charming stone houses and cozy cafes. The local people are very welcoming and eager to share stories about the region's rich history and cultural heritage.

If you're an adventurous traveler, consider taking a boat trip on the Buna River for a one-of-a-kind view of the spring and its beautiful surroundings. As you drift along the serene waters, you can admire the way the light reflects off the surface, producing a beautiful array of colors that dance with the reflections of the cliffs and foliage, creating a constantly shifting masterpiece. The Buna region is not just a visual delight, but also a paradise for food lovers. Experience the authentic flavors of Bosnian cuisine at neighborhood eateries, with a menu showcasing classics such as cevapi, burek, and freshly grilled fish from the pure waters of the Buna River. Eating outside while listening to the springtime sounds creates a lasting memory.

If you want to truly experience the peace and serenity of Buna Spring, you should think about booking a stay at one of the lovely guesthouses that are scattered throughout the area. Rise and shine to the tranquil melodies of nature, savor a delightful cup of Bosnian coffee while taking in the view of the spring from the terrace, and allow the relaxed and leisurely lifestyle in Blagaj to revive your soul. Buna Spring in Blagaj is not just your average destination, it's a perfect mix of stunning natural beauty, cultural abundance, and welcoming hospitality.

Trebinje

The Tvrdos Monastery, which dates back to the 15th century, is a peaceful sanctuary situated along the tranquil banks of the Trebisnjica River. The name "Tvrdos" translates to "hard" or "firm" in English, which reflects the steadfast and enduring spirit of the monastery that has endured the passage of time. The monastery's architecture combines Byzantine and medieval styles to create a visually striking and spiritually evocative atmosphere. The monastery is known for its exceptional vineyards, which yield some of the best wines in the area.

For centuries, the monks of Tvrdos have been growing grapes and preserving ancient winemaking customs that have been handed down from generation to generation. Guests can leisurely walk through the vineyards, gain insights into the art of winemaking, and savor the delightful flavors of regional wines during tastings. The spiritual significance of the monastery is firmly embedded in its long history. The monastery's interior is embellished with stunning frescoes and religious iconography, offering a peek into the region's rich religious and artistic legacy.

If you're looking for a peaceful getaway, Tvrdos Monastery provides a calm courtyard and gardens for visitors to relax and reflect in quiet solitude. The tranquil environment makes it a perfect place for photography, enabling visitors to capture the enduring beauty of this historic site. In order to improve the experience for visitors, the monastery from time to time holds cultural events and religious ceremonies.

If you're thinking of visiting Tvrdos Monastery, don't forget to explore the beautiful surroundings of Trebinje. The town has charming cobblestone streets, historic architecture, and a bustling local market. The Tvrdos experience goes beyond the monastery, providing a thorough exploration of the cultural and natural marvels that characterize this charming area of Bosnia and Herzegovina. The Tvrdos Monastery in Trebinje is more than just a historical site - it stands as a testament to the enduring spirit of tradition and community.

The Arslanagića Bridge exudes timeless elegance as you near it, capturing your attention immediately. The bridge is made of local stone and showcases the skill and artistry of craftsmen from long ago. As you walk across the sturdy arches, you can almost sense the whispers of history resonating in the air. The bridge is not just a means of crossing the river; it is also a tribute to the influential Arslanagića family, who left their mark on the region's history. It stands as a silent observer of the stories of merchants, voyagers, and residents who have journeyed along its route throughout the years.

When standing at the center of the Arslanagića Bridge, you can enjoy breathtaking panoramic vistas of Trebinje's landscape. The clear blue sky is mirrored by the river below, adding to the bridge's allure with its mesmerizing reflection. This place is a peaceful oasis where time appears to pause, giving guests the opportunity to fully appreciate the stunning hills and the rich history of Trebinje. If you want a more immersive experience, you can enjoy a leisurely walk along the nearby cobblestone streets. The Arslanagića Bridge serves as more than just a bridge - it's a portal to Trebinje's historic old town, inviting you to discover charming cafes, bustling markets, and significant landmarks. As the sun sinks below the horizon, enveloping the Arslanagića Bridge in a warm glow, the atmosphere takes on a magical quality.

The lights that shine on the bridge make for a stunning scene, perfect for photographers and hopeless romantics. It's a picture-perfect spot for both. As the sun sets in Trebinje, the bridge becomes a timeless symbol of beauty. As you travel through Bosnia and Herzegovina, the

Arslanagića Bridge in Trebinje serves as a testament to the diverse and vibrant history and culture of the country. The bridge is more than just a structure; it represents a link to history, a captivating sight, and a must-see spot for those wanting to uncover the essence of this captivating area.

Exploring Nature

Plitvice Lakes National Park

The Plitvice Lakes National Park lies in the heart of Croatia, near the border with Bosnia and Herzegovina, and is a true natural gem. The UNESCO World Heritage site is famous for its stunning natural scenery, mesmerizing waterfalls, and unspoiled lakes. Get ready for an incredible immersion in nature's beauty as you journey from Bosnia and Herzegovina to Plitvice Lakes. The beautiful waters, displaying shades from azure to emerald, are evidence of the park's captivating charm. The sight of Veliki Slap, the biggest waterfall in the park, is truly impressive.

The rumbling waters reverberate through the valley, leaving visitors awe-struck by the majesty of nature. The park provides a network of wooden pathways and hiking trails for those wanting a more intimate exploration, allowing visitors to meander through the diverse landscapes. The flora and fauna are both incredibly fascinating, offering habitat to a wide range of plant and animal species. Make sure to watch for the rare lynx, brown bear, and many types of birds that live in the park. If you want to enhance your visit, think about taking a boat trip across Lake Kozjak. The peaceful boat journey offers a distinctive view of the park's stunning scenery. Moreover, the park features strategically placed panoramic viewpoints that provide breathtaking vistas, allowing visitors to capture the true essence of Plitvice Lakes. As you explore the core of this breathtaking natural wonder, you'll uncover the interlocking network of lakes and waterfalls, forming an ecosystem that is both fragile and strong. The park is dedicated to conservation and urges visitors to preserve the pristine environment by staying on designated paths and following guidelines.

To fully enjoy the experience, consider visiting during various seasons. The colors of Plitvice Lakes change with the weather, showcasing a variety of hues in the fall, a snowy paradise in winter, and bursting with vibrant flowers in the spring and summer. The park is easy to reach from Bosnia and Herzegovina, with plenty of transportation choices. Make sure to carefully plan your visit, taking into account the weather and the volume of people, in order to ensure a smooth and pleasant experience. To sum up, Plitvice Lakes National Park showcases the unmatched beauty that nature has to offer.

While discovering its marvels, you will not just see a beautiful show of water and plants but also develop a greater understanding of the fragile harmony that supports this ecological work of art. Get ready for an unforgettable journey into the heart of one of Europe's most captivating natural wonders. Lace up your hiking boots, pack your camera, and prepare for an adventure like no other.

Una National Park

Located in the heart of Bosnia and Herzegovina, Una National Park is an untouched gem that invites travelers to a world of untouched natural beauty. Established in 2008, this fascinating park spans the rivers Una, Krka and Unac, creating a picturesque landscape with dense forests, waterfalls and a seamless mix of diverse flora and fauna. The crown jewel of the park is the Una River, known for its crystal-clear turquoise water and lively rapids. As you explore the park, you will encounter the magnificent Una Falls, a mesmerizing waterfall that plunges into several pools, creating an enchanting environment to relax and admire nature and wonders.

The sound of flowing water and the smell of pine trees create a sensual experience that is truly unforgettable. Adventurers will find plenty of opportunities for outdoor activities, including hiking trails that wind through dense forests and offer stunning panoramic views of the surrounding mountains. Una National Park is also a paradise for wildlife lovers, where you can see brown bears, wolves and various bird species in their natural habitat. For those looking for a more peaceful experience, the park offers quiet spots along the river banks where you can enjoy a quiet picnic or simply enjoy the tranquility of the unspoiled surroundings. The Una region is also rich in cultural heritage, with nearby medieval castles and traditional Bosnian villages offering a glimpse into the country and its rich history.

The town of Bihac, close to the park, is an excellent base for exploring Una National Park. With charming cafes, historic architecture and warm hospitality, Bihac offers a delightful blend of urban comfort and nature. While traveling in Una National Park, take time to interact with local communities, sample traditional Bosnian cuisine and immerse yourself in the tapestry of culture that characterizes this unique region. Whether you are an avid adventurer or a peace seeker, Una National Park welcomes you with open arms, promising an authentic and enriching experience in the heart of Bosnia and Herzegovina.

Vrelo Bosne

On the outskirts of Sarajevo, the capital of Bosnia and Herzegovina, lies an enchanting oasis known as Vrelo Bosne. The charming natural wonder of Vrelo Bosne is a destination that perfectly combines the tranquility of nature with the rich history of the region. As you make your way to this hidden gem, be prepared to immerse yourself in the amazing beauty that unfolds before your eyes. Vrelo Bosne is celebrated for its unspoilt springs, where the Bosna River rises from under the greenery of Mount Igman. As soon as you set foot in this idyllic setting, you are greeted by the soothing sounds of water flowing through the vibrant vegetation.

Crystal clear streams meander through the park, creating a peaceful atmosphere that invites visitors to relax and connect with nature. One of the highlights of Vrelo Bosne is the Vrelo Bosne Springs, the source of the Bosna River. Take a leisurely stroll through the park along the well-maintained paths that lead to these iconic springs. Admire the clarity of the water gushing up from the depths, creating a mesmerizing reflection of the surrounding trees and hills. The air is filled with the refreshing scent of pine, enhancing the sensory experience.

While exploring the park, don't miss the opportunity to visit Velika Aleja, a large street lined with towering chestnut trees. This majestic tree-lined avenue is especially enchanting during the spring season, when chestnut blossoms adorn the branches, creating a mesmerizing canopy of shades of pink and white. It is the perfect place for a leisurely stroll where you can admire the beauty of your surroundings. For those looking for a moment of tranquility, the park offers charming wooden bridges that cross gentle streams. Find a quiet place to sit and meditate and let the sounds of nature and babbling streams transport you to a peaceful space. It is a place where time seems to stand still, allowing visitors to escape the hustle and bustle of everyday life.

Vrelo Bosne is not only a haven for nature lovers, but also a historically important destination. The park includes Atmejdan Park, where you can explore the remains of a medieval settlement and the famous Atmejdan Cemetery. These historical landmarks offer a glimpse into Bosnia and Herzegovina's rich tapestry and past, adding depth to your visit.

To make the most of your experience, consider packing a picnic and eating amidst the natural beauty of Vrelo Bosne.

The park has several picnic areas with tables and benches, so you can enjoy local delicacies surrounded by stunning scenery. Vrelo Bosne is a sign of the harmonious coexistence of nature and history. Whether you're a nature lover, a history buff or someone just looking for a peaceful getaway, this enchanting destination has something for everyone. As you explore the winding roads of Vrelo Bosne and discover hidden treasures, you will find yourself on a journey of beauty, peace and cultural richness that is uniquely Bosnian.

Sutjeska National Park

A true gem in the heart of Bosnia and Herzegovina, Sutjeska National Park offers a fascinating mix of natural beauty, rich history and an unparalleled outdoor environment. Located in the southeastern part of the country, this national park is a testament to the diverse and fascinating landscapes of Bosnia and Herzegovina.

Encompassing the majestic peaks of the Dinaric Alps, Sutjeska National Park is a haven for nature lovers and adventure seekers alike. The park is home to Bosnia and Herzegovina's highest peak, Maglić, which stands proudly at 2,386 meters above sea level. Trails criss-cross the park, leading intrepid explorers through dense forests, past crystal-clear mountain streams and breathtaking viewpoints with panoramic views of the surrounding desert.

One of the crown jewels of the park is the pristine Perućica Forest Reserve, one of the last primeval forests in Europe. Walking under towering trees and abundant vegetation, visitors can experience a truly untouched natural environment where flora and fauna have been preserved for centuries. The rustle of leaves and the voices of songbirds create a symphony of nature that offers a peaceful and refreshing escape from the hustle and bustle of everyday life.

History buffs will find Sutjeska National Park equally fascinating as it played an important role during World War II. In 1943, the battle of Sutjeska took place here, which is one of the biggest and most important battles in the region. The memorial complex, including the iconic Sutjeska Battle Memorial, is a poignant reminder of the sacrifices made during this turbulent time. Visiting the historical sites of the park offers a unique perspective on the determination and courage of the people of Bosnia and Herzegovina.

For those looking for a more active activity, the Tara River, known for its emerald green waters, offers exciting opportunities for rafting and kayaking. The river meanders through a deep canyon, creating an adrenaline-pumping adventure in the midst of amazing nature.

Accommodations in and around Sutjeska National Park suit a variety of preferences, from cozy mountain cabins to campsites for those who want to fully immerse themselves in the great outdoors. The local cuisine, influenced by the region and agricultural traditions, presents rich and delicious dishes that are sure to satisfy your appetite after a day of exploring.

Sutjeska National Park is a destination where the peace of untouched nature blends perfectly with the historical significance of the central wartime past. Whether you're an avid hiker, history buff or just someone looking for a peaceful escape, this national park offers an unforgettable experience that captures the essence of Bosnia and Herzegovina and its natural and cultural heritage.

Kravica Waterfalls

Kravica waterfalls are a testament to the nature that adorns this area. These green waterfalls of the Studenc River are a hidden gem that avid travelers await. When you go to the falls, the trip itself becomes a mesmerizing experience. The roads wind through charming villages, offering a glimpse of traditional Bosnian life. Upon arrival, the roar of the waterfall intensifies, adding to the amazing sight that awaits. Looking at Kravica Waterfall, it's hard not to fall in love with the natural splendor and handiwork. The waterfalls and their emerald green pools create an enchanting landscape against the backdrop of the dense forest.

Water flows from different heights, creating a symphony of soothing sounds that reverberate through the air. During the summer months, Kravica turns into an idyllic paradise. The pools at the foot of the waterfall invite visitors to refresh and offer respite from the hot Bosnian sun. The surrounding meadows provide the perfect place for a peaceful picnic where you can enjoy the tranquility of the surroundings. For those looking for a more adventurous experience, exploring the trails around Kravica is a must. Trails led through the heart of untouched nature and open up panoramic views of the falls from different vantage points. An immersive experience surrounded by the sights and sounds of the desert will add magic to your trip.

If you want to really appreciate the Kravica Waterfall, consider visiting during the quieter times of the day. Early mornings or late afternoons offer a more intimate encounter with the falls, allowing you to enjoy the tranquility without the crowds.

As you explore this natural wonder, take a moment to reflect on the rich cultural and historical tapestry of Bosnia and Herzegovina. Kravica waterfalls with their timeless beauty testify to the harmony of nature and the human spirit in this enchanting corner of the world. Basically, the Kravica Falls promise not only a visual spectacle, but a full sensory experience, making them a must-stop for any traveler through Bosnia and Herzegovina. As you admire the waters, you will discover the beauty and serenity of this fascinating destination.

Get your FREE book

Please visit https://tinyurl.com/travel-with-jeffery for additional resources and to engage with my newsletter.

I also want to reward you for purchasing my book. To get the reward which is a travel planner; kindly click on this link below or open the link on your browser.

https://tinyurl.com/travel-with-jeffery

I hope you love the travel planner!

Embracing Culture and History

In this exploration, we delve into the historical and heritage aspects of Bosnian culture, with a particular focus on the Ottoman and Austro-Hungarian eras, as well as the more recent and tumultuous chapter in the nation's history – the Bosnian War.

Bosnia has profound historical roots, with the Ottoman Empire's four-century presence being one of the most significant chapters. The Ottomans left an indelible mark on Bosnian architecture, gastronomy, and social institutions beginning in the late 15th century. Stroll through Sarajevo's cobblestone streets, where the elaborate designs of the Sebilj fountain and the Gazi Husrev-beg Mosque reflect the echoes of Ottoman craftsmanship.

Following the Ottoman era in the late nineteenth century, the Austro-Hungarian period brought a new wave of influences. Austro-Hungarian architecture changed urban landscapes, leaving attractive buildings in locations such as Mostar. During this period, the blend of Eastern and Western influences is perceptible in Bosnian cuisine, as traditional Bosnian dishes coexist alongside Viennese pastries and coffee culture.

With the commencement of the Bosnian War (1992-1995), the late twentieth century brought a gloomy chapter to Bosnia and Herzegovina. This conflict, which arose as a result of Yugoslavia's collapse, had a long-lasting impact on the nation's identity and people. Visit the War Childhood Museum in Sarajevo to obtain a vivid understanding of Bosnian children's lives during this terrible period. The scars of battle may be seen in bullet-riddled buildings and remnants of the Siege of Sarajevo, reminding tourists of the Bosnian people's endurance and strength.

While the war had its consequences, Bosnia and Herzegovina emerged from the shadows determined to rebuild and redefine its identity. Today, the cities are testaments to the people's resilient spirit, mixing the scars of the past with a lively and hopeful present.

The cultural journey of Bosnia and Herzegovina is one of perseverance, adaptation, and the harmonious coexistence of many influences. The nation encourages travelers to go on a profound exploration of history and legacy, from the grandeur of Ottoman buildings to the beauty of Austro-Hungarian designs and the gloomy echoes of the Bosnian War.

You'll discover a nation that embraces its past while looking forward to a future full of hope and possibilities as you walk the streets and absorb the stories ingrained in the fabric of Bosnia.

Bosnian Traditions

Bosnian traditions, from ancient rites to modern festivities, provide tourists with a one-of-a-kind and authentic experience. Let's look at some significant features of Bosnian traditions that you might be interested in.

1. Bosnians are well-known for their warm hospitality, and they treat visitors with genuine compassion and generosity. Expect to be greeted with wide arms and offered traditional Bosnian coffee, a symbol of hospitality, when visiting a Bosnian home. Heartfelt talks over coffee are a treasured practice that fosters a sense of connection and fraternity.

2. Bosnian cuisine is a delectable fusion of Ottoman, Austro-Hungarian, and Balkan influences, resulting in a one-of-a-kind culinary experience. The staples of the country's gastronomic diversity include evapi, a type of grilled minced meat, and burek, a savory pastry filled with meat, cheese, or spinach. Don't pass up the chance to sample Bosnian cuisine in local restaurants and homes.

3. Sevdah, sometimes known as "Bosnian Blues," is a traditional Bosnian music genre that captures the lyrical essence of Bosnian life. Sevdah, with its melancholy melodies and passionate lyrics, expresses the joys and tragedies of ordinary life. Attending a live Sevdah

performance provides a deep dive into Bosnian culture's emotional essence.

4. Bosnia and Herzegovina is noted for its peaceful coexistence of several religious communities, most notably Islam, Orthodox Christianity, and Catholicism. Tolerance is represented by the unique practice of celebrating religious festivals together, which fosters togetherness and understanding among people of different faiths.

5. Bosnia and Herzegovina come alive with vivid festivals and celebrations all year. The Sarajevo Film Festival attracts filmmakers and film aficionados from all over the world, while religious festivals such as Bajram (Eid) and Christmas are celebrated with zeal, providing visitors with a view into the country's cultural tapestry.

6. Bosnian craftsmanship is steeped in tradition, with talented artisans creating complex handcrafted items. Discover wonderfully crafted copperware, traditional rugs, and elaborately decorated woodwork in bustling bazaars and markets. Buying these things not only helps local artists but also provides as a concrete memento of your trip to Bosnia.

Stari Most, Mostar's iconic bridge, represents solidarity and resilience. The daring act of diving is an age-old custom associated with the bridge. Locals, known as "mostari," demonstrate their daring by leaping from the bridge into the Neretva River, creating a spectacle that captivates visitors and adds an adrenaline-fueled element to the city's environment.

Incorporating these diverse traditions into your Bosnia and Herzegovina travel guide will surely help readers better comprehend the country's cultural tapestry.

Festivals and Events

Bosnia and Herzegovina, with its rich cultural tapestry and stunning surroundings, is not just a historical destination, but also a bustling hub for festivals and events that highlight the nation's soul. The Sarajevo Film Festival and the Mostar Summer Fest are two notable celebrations that reflect the heart of Bosnian innovation and friendliness.

Sarajevo Film Festival

During the famed Sarajevo Film Festival, the capital city of Sarajevo transforms into a cinematic wonderland every summer. This event, which began in 1995, has evolved to become one of the most prestigious film festivals in Southeast Europe, attracting directors, actors, and film aficionados from all over the world.

The festival's principal goal is to present outstanding films that explore varied topics and push the boundaries of cinematic expression. From thought-provoking documentaries to captivating feature films, the Sarajevo Film Festival curates a program that embodies Bosnia and Herzegovina's cultural richness and tenacity.

The festival's primary focus is on showing excellent films that explore varied topics and push the boundaries of cinematic expression. From thought-provoking documentaries to captivating feature films, the Sarajevo Film Festival curates a program that embodies Bosnia and Herzegovina's cultural richness and resilience.

Beyond the screen, the event produces an exciting environment in Sarajevo's center. The old city streets come alive with a mix of red-carpet elegance, busy markets, and open-air movies, providing both locals and visitors with an unforgettable experience. It is more than just a film festival; it is a celebration of storytelling, culture, and the resilient spirit of the Bosnian people.

Mostar Summer Fest

Mostar Summer Fest offers a unique and magical experience for those looking for a different flavor of cultural celebration. This summer festival lends a dynamic touch to the historic surroundings of Mostar, which is known for its distinctive bridge and Ottoman architecture.

Mostar Summer Fest is a multi-disciplinary celebration of art, music, and performance set against the breathtaking backdrop of Mostar's landmarks. The festival's broad program includes open-air concerts by local and international performers, art displays highlighting the region's creative ability, and dramatic performances that bring Mostar's ancient streets to life.

The combination of traditional Bosnian music with current sounds is one of the festival's highlights, creating a melodic bridge between the past and the present. Visitors may expect to be taken away by the rhythmic pulses resonating throughout the city, creating an amazing environment that will stay with them long after the festival has over.

The Sarajevo Film Festival and the Mostar Summer Fest, located in the heart of Bosnia and Herzegovina, are lively testaments to the country's artistic vitality and endurance. These festivals welcome you with open arms, whether you are a cinephile looking for the newest in world cinema or an art enthusiast looking for a one-of-a-kind cultural experience.

As you walk through Sarajevo's streets during the film festival or immerse yourself in the artistic tapestry of Mostar's summer celebration, you'll learn that these events are more than just gatherings; they are representations of the tenacious human spirit that defines Bosnia and Herzegovina. If you embrace the charm of these festivals, you will be knitted into the rich cultural fabric of this magnificent country.

Bosnian Arts and Crafts

Exploring Bosnian arts and crafts offers a unique glimpse into the essence of this intriguing country, where influences from the East and the West meet to form a distinct and engaging artistic history.

The art of sevdah, a traditional musical genre profoundly established in Bosnian culture, is one of the most visible manifestations of Bosnian craftsmanship. Sevdah embodies the essence of the Bosnian spirit with its melancholy tunes and sincere lyrics. It is frequently accompanied with the soul-stirring melodies of the saz, a stringed instrument that gives a particular resonance to the musical experience. As you walk through the cobblestone streets of Sarajevo or Mostar, you may hear echoes of sevdah in cafes, houses, and public areas, highlighting Bosnians' great emotional attachment to their musical legacy.

Bosnia and Herzegovina's cultural history may also be seen in its expert workmanship, most notably in the production of traditional Bosnian carpets. These carpets are handcrafted by experienced artisans using skills passed down through centuries and are noted for their intricate designs and brilliant colors. Each carpet tells a story, intertwining the strands of Bosnian history from the

Ottoman period to the present. These works are more than just beautiful; they are indicative of the Bosnian people's tenacity and inventiveness.

Another art form that is profoundly ingrained in Bosnian culture is woodcarving. Skilled woodworkers carve exquisite motifs into furniture, sacred relics, and even daily items, resulting in practical and aesthetically beautiful pieces. The carvings' combination of Islamic geometric patterns with Christian motifs reflects Bosnia and Herzegovina's religious and cultural diversity.

Bosnian artists demonstrate their talent in the field of pottery by crafting one-of-a-kind and exquisite ceramic items. Tuzla, with its centuries-old pottery-making heritage, is a mecca for those looking for real Bosnian ceramics. Bosnian pottery, from finely painted plates to robust yet attractive kitchenware, illustrates the country's commitment to conserving its artistic past while adapting to modern demands.

When you visit Bosnia and Herzegovina's bazaars and markets, you'll find a wealth of handcrafted gifts that serve as physical recollections of your adventure. Hand-knit woolens, delicately embroidered linens, and leather products embellished with traditional Bosnian motifs are just a few of the treasures available for purchase.

As you explore Bosnia and Herzegovina's arts and crafts, you will find not just the ability and creativity of its artists, but also the fundamental relationship between art and identity. Whether it's a musical composition, a woven carpet, or a carved wooden decoration, each piece adds to the mosaic of Bosnian culture, enabling visitors to immerse themselves in the distinctive and enchanting world of Bosnian arts and crafts.

Handicrafts and Souvenirs

Purchasing locally created handicrafts and special souvenirs while seeing Bosnia and Herzegovina's diverse culture can be a pleasant way to recall your journey. Here are some genuine recommendations that reflect this magnificent country's rich heritage:

Sarajevo's Bascarsija Bazaar:

The Bascarsija Bazaar, located in the heart of Sarajevo, is a treasure trove of handcrafted items. Wander through its cobblestone lanes dotted with small stores to find a variety of traditional Bosnian products such as finely crafted copperware, colorful rugs, and unique wooden items. Engage with local craftsmen, and you could even get to see these beauties being created firsthand.

Etno Art Shop, Jajce:

Jajce, with its stunning waterfall and historic fortress, is also a popular destination for traditional Bosnian handicrafts. Etno Art Shop, located in the town center, offers a broad selection of handmade goods such as textiles, leather items, and ethno-style accessories. The shop's dedication to encouraging local handicraft assures that its items are genuine.

Mostar and Sarajevo Local Markets:

Explore the busy markets of Mostar and Sarajevo to completely immerse yourself in the local culture. These marketplaces, such as Sarajevo's Markale Market, are a kaleidoscope of colors and scents. Vendors sell a wide range of handmade goods, from embroidered linens to aromatic spices. Engaging with the sellers provides a genuine experience as well as an opportunity to learn more about the artistry that goes into each piece.

Remember that the core of Bosnian and Herzegovina's handicrafts rests not only in the items themselves, but also in the stories that go with them. Supporting local artisans and marketplaces not only allows you to bring home unique and meaningful gifts, but it also helps to preserve Bosnia and Herzegovina's cultural heritage.

Traditional Music and Dance

Traditional music and dance play an important part in expressing Bosnia and Herzegovina's spirit and cultural identity, and one of the most compelling interpretations of this rich history may be found in the soul-stirring melodies of Sevdalinka music. Sevdalinka, a folk music genre profoundly established in Bosnian history, transcends time, engaging with people's hearts and stories.

Sevdalinka, which is derived from the Turkish word "sevda," which means "love or passion," encompasses a wide spectrum of emotions, from love and joy to melancholy and despair. The music frequently includes hauntingly beautiful melodies accompanied by meaningful lyrics, resulting in an emotional experience for both the performers and the listeners.

One cannot enter the realm of Sevdalinka without first understanding its historical significance. This musical genre, which originated during the Ottoman era, has evolved over the years, absorbing diverse influences and reflecting the region's vast cultural tapestry. The lyrics, which are commonly sung in Bosnian, depict themes of love, sorrow, and everyday challenges, offering a heartbreaking narrative of the Bosnian experience.

Sevdalinka is distinguished by the use of traditional folk instruments such as the saz, a stringed instrument with a characteristic pear-shaped body, and the accordion. When these instruments are played well, they give a dimension of authenticity to the song, bringing listeners to a different time and place.

Beyond the auditory experience, Sevdalinka is deeply linked to traditional Bosnian dancing. The beautiful and expressive dance moves echo the emotional intricacies of the song. Dancers frequently use traditional garb that is embellished with vivid colors and ornate designs, giving a visual spectacle to the performance.

Attending a live performance is the only way to really immerse oneself in the world of Sevdalinka. Whether in a small café or a vast concert hall, the interaction between performers and audience provides a community experience that goes beyond simply entertainment. It becomes a shared cultural festival and a monument to the Bosnian spirit's tenacity.

Make it a point to look for locations and events that include Sevdalinka while you travel through Bosnia and Herzegovina. The echoes of this ageless music may be heard throughout the country, from Sarajevo's old streets to the picturesque settlements buried in the hills. Interact with locals, listen to their experiences, and let the evocative notes of Sevdalinka to weave a thread linking you to the heart and soul of Bosnia and Herzegovina's cultural legacy.

Culinary Adventures

Bosnian Cuisine

The culinary traditions of Bosnia and Herzegovina are a unique combination of Ottoman, Austro-Hungarian, and Balkan flavors, resulting in a gastronomic experience that is both distinct and satisfying. One of the cornerstone factors of Bosnian cuisine is its highlighting on fresh, locally sourced ingredients. From the fertile plains to the pristine rivers, the country's geography contributes to the high quality and authenticity of its food.

The use of seasonal produce and classical farming techniques imparts a genuine and wholesome character to Bosnian dishes. At the center of Bosnian cuisine is a love for grilled meats, reflecting the impact of Ottoman culinary practices. evapi, small [tiny] minced meat sausages, are a quintessential Bosnian dish often enjoyed with somun, a soft and airy flatbread. This simple yet flavorful combination is a staple street food and can be found at local eateries known as evabdinicas.

In addition to grilled meats, Bosnian cuisine boasts a variety of stews, soups, and hearty casseroles. Bey's soup (Begova orba), a velvety mix [mixture, combination, fusion, blend] of chicken, okra, and spices, exemplifies the fusion of Ottoman and local flavors. One dish that demonstrates the influence of Turkish cuisine is called "sogan-dolma," which is made of rice and minced meat packed inside onions. The variety of Bosnian pastries and sweets is also apparent in their cuisine. Baklava is a treat that originated in the Ottoman Empire. It is a dessert made of layered filo pastry, chopped nuts, and honey or syrup for sweetness.

A delightful combination of flavors and textures can be found in Tufahija, a Bosnian specialty made with poached quince topped with cream and walnuts. Without mentioning Bosnian coffee, no discussion of Bosnian food would be complete. Bosnian coffee is traditionally sipped slowly, among friends, and as a ritual that promotes interaction.

The coffee's robust, rich flavor serves as a reminder of how important it is to live in the present and enjoy life's finer things. Make sure to experience the regional cuisine when traveling through Bosnia and Herzegovina. Experience the warmth of Bosnian hospitality and savor dishes that tell the story of this remarkable country by dining at traditional establishments, or konobas. Bosnian food is a flavor journey that will surely leave a lasting impression on any traveler's palate, from the vibrant markets of Sarajevo to the charming villages nestled away in the countryside.

Must-Try Dishes

Here are some must-try dishes that will tantalize your taste buds:

1. **Evapi:** Bosnian Grilled Minced Meat A culinary icon of Bosnia, evapi are small, hand-rolled minced meat sausages, typically made from a of beef and lamb. Grilled to perfection and served with somun (flatbread), diced onions, and a dollop of kajmak (clotted cream), this dish is a true celebration of smoky, savory goodness.

2. **Begova orba**: Bey's Soup Prepare your palate for a taste of Ottoman sophistication with Begova orba. This velvety soup, also known as Bey's Soup, combines okra, chicken, and an assortment of vegetables, creating a harmonious blend of textures and flavors. It's a historical delicacy that whispers tales of the Ottoman era.

3. **Japrak**: Stuffed Grape Leaves Japrak is a dish that showcases the artistry of Bosnian home cooking. Grape leaves are carefully stuffed with a tantalizing mixture of ground meat, rice, and spices, creating bite-sized parcels

bursting with flavor. Often served with a side of yogurt, Japrak is a true taste of traditional Bosnian hospitality.

4. **Pita**: Bosnian Pie Bosnian Pita, a flaky pastry filled with layers of minced meat, cheese, or potatoes, takes center stage at Bosnian tables. The aroma of freshly baked Pita wafting through the air is an irresistible invitation to indulge in this savory delight, often enjoyed as a hearty snack or a fulfilling meal.

5. **Burek**: Balkan Savory Pastry No culinary journey through Bosnia & Herzegovina is complete without savoring Burek. Layers of thin dough are meticulously filled with minced meat, cheese, or spinach, creating a savory spiral that delights both the eyes and the taste buds. Pair it with a dollop of yogurt for the perfect balance.

6. **Sogan-dolma**: Stuffed Onions Sogan-dolma, or stuffed onions, is a dish that showcases the ingenuity of Bosnian cuisine. Onions are hollowed out and filled with a mixture of meat, rice, and spices before being slow-cooked to perfection. The result is a savory, aromatic dish that captures the essence of Bosnian comfort food.

7. **Tufahija**: Poached Walnut-Stuffed Apples For those with a sweet tooth, Tufahija is a dessert that promises a

symphony of flavors. Poached apples are stuffed with walnuts and sugar, then topped with whipped cream, creating a decadent treat that reflects the rich culinary heritage of Bosnia & Herzegovina. In Bosnia, every dish tells a story, and each bite is a journey through centuries of tradition.

So, as you explore the charming streets and landscapes of this beautiful country, don't miss the opportunity to savor the authentic flavors that make Bosnian cuisine truly unforgettable.

Popular Local Restaurants

Here are some popular local restaurants that encapsulate the essence of Bosnian cuisine:

Evabdinica Petica: Located in the heart of Sarajevo, evabdinica Petica is a beloved spot for locals and visitors alike. This unassuming eatery specializes in evapi, a traditional Bosnian dish consisting of grilled minced meat, typically served with somun (a type of flatbread), chopped onions, and red pepper sauce. The rustic charm of the restaurant and the mouthwatering aroma of grilled meat make it a must-visit.

Inat Kua: Situated on the banks of the Miljacka River, Inat Kua is a historic restaurant with a story as compelling as its menu. Originally built as an act of defiance against city planners during the Austro-Hungarian rule, the restaurant serves up a delectable selection of Bosnian dishes. Guests can enjoy local specialties like japrak (stuffed grape leaves) and dolma in a setting that seamlessly blends tradition with modernity.

Begova Damija Courtyard: Tucked within the courtyard of the iconic Gazi Husrev-beg Mosque in Sarajevo's Baarija district, this restaurant offers an enchanting dining experience. Known for its tranquil ambiance and breathtaking views, the Begova Damija Courtyard serves classic Bosnian fare. Indulge in dishes like Bosanski lonac (Bosnian pot), a slow-cooked stew of meat and vegetables, while immersed in the historical charm of the surroundings.

Evabinica Hodi: A family-run gem in Mostar, evabinica Hodi is celebrated for its dedication to traditional recipes and warm hospitality. The restaurant's courtyard, adorned with vibrant flowers, provides an inviting setting to savor local delicacies. Don't miss out on the mantije, a Bosnian pastry filled with minced meat, onions, and spices, offering a delightful burst of flavors with every bite.

Sadrvan: Nestled in the heart of Banja Luka, Sadrvan is a culinary haven for those seeking an authentic taste of Bosnian cuisine. The menu boasts a variety of dishes, including the iconic Bosanski evapi and the hearty grah, a bean soup infused with smoked meat. The restaurant's cozy interior and friendly staff create a welcoming atmosphere, making it a favorite among locals.

Kod Bibana: For a truly local experience in Tuzla, Kod Bibana stands out as a popular choice. Famous for its sogan-dolma—onions filled with perfectly cooked rice and minced meat—this quaint eatery is well-known for its food. Kod Bibana is a fun place to visit if you're checking out

Tuzla's food options because of its laid-back vibe and blend of modern and traditional elements. Indulge in the flavors of these well-known regional eateries to start your culinary journey through Bosnia and Herzegovina.

Street Food Delights

From the bustling markets of Sarajevo to the quaint alleys of Mostar, the street food scene in Bosnia and Herzegovina offers a diverse array of flavors that reflect the country's history, traditions, and the warmth of its people.

Evapi - Grilled Bliss: Begin your culinary exploration with a quintessential Bosnian delight - evapi. These small, grilled minced meat sausages, typically made from a blend of beef and lamb, are a ubiquitous street food favourite. Served with somun (a type of flatbread), chopped onions, and a dollop of kajmak (clotted cream), evapi embodies the perfect balance of smoky, savory goodness.

Burek - A Flaky Indulgence: As you meander through the labyrinthine streets, the aroma of freshly baked Burek wafting from local bakeries will undoubtedly beckon you. This flaky pastry, filled with minced meat, cheese, or spinach, is a beloved snack enjoyed by locals and visitors alike. Pair it with a side of yogurt for an authentic Bosnian experience.

Grasping Grilled Corn: During your street food odyssey, you'll likely encounter vendors selling grilled corn on the cob, a popular choice among locals. The corn is carefully grilled until golden brown, then seasoned with salt, pepper, and a dash of lemon. This is a simple yet delicious dish that epitomizes Bosnian street cuisine.

Exploring Bosnian Street food is an absolute must, and Ćufte is a must-try. These fried and seasoned meatballs are a delicious way to experience the country's culinary mastery. They are usually served with mashed potatoes or ajvar, a red pepper-based condiment. For those with a love of cheese, Sirnica is a must-have. This pastry is filled with a blend of cottage cheese and eggs, and is a savory treat that captures the essence of Bosnian cuisine. It's a great snack to enjoy while taking in the stunning scenery of Bosnia and Herzegovina. From the smoky Ćevapi to the flaky layers of Burek, the street food of this country is a journey for the senses, showcasing the culinary artistry that has been passed down through generations.

Outdoor Activities

Hiking and Trekking

A hidden gem for hiking enthusiasts, Bosnia and Herzegovina offers a diverse landscape where nature, culture and adventure merge seamlessly. From the rugged peaks of the Dinaric Alps to the unspoiled beauty of its national parks, the country invites explorers on a journey that goes beyond ordinary travel. Take the epic Via Dinarica route through the Balkans, from bustling Sarajevo in Bosnia and Herzegovina to the charming city of Mostar. This route showcases the country and its rich cultural background and provides a mesmerizing backdrop of towering peaks, dense forests and serene lakes.

Enter the wilderness of Sutjeska National Park, home to Bosnia and Herzegovina's highest peak, Mount Maglić. The park has diverse flora and fauna, making it a paradise for nature lovers. A challenging ride to the top offers adventurers a panoramic view that stretches all the way to Montenegro. For a peaceful hike, head to Una National Park, where the Una River flows through lush greenery. Hiking along the banks of the river offers a unique combination of untouched nature and the opportunity to see diverse nature. The Una Vojo promises an immersive experience with waterfalls and canyons creating a picturesque backdrop.

The versatile climate of Bosnia and Herzegovina guarantees an exciting experience throughout the year. Spring and fall offer mild temperatures, making them ideal for most hikers. Summer invites adventurers to explore higher elevations, while winter transforms the landscape into a winter wonderland for those looking for a snow hiking adventure.

Rafting on the Neretva River

Rafting on the Neretva River is an exciting adventure that offers a unique blend of natural beauty and adrenaline-pumping excitement. Located in the heart of Bosnia and Herzegovina, the Neretva River flows through stunning landscapes, making it a must experience for adventure seekers and nature lovers.

The journey begins in the picturesque village of Konjic, where eager rafters gather to begin an exciting journey through the river and crystal-clear water. As you sail, the emerald green surroundings of the Neretva Valley provide a stunning backdrop, creating the feeling of being in the unspoiled Bosnian wilderness.

The Neretva River is known for its various rapids, which range from gentle currents that allow you to enjoy the scenery in peace, to challenging sections that will test your rafting skills. Different levels of difficulty make this adventure suitable for both beginners and experienced keyboard players, ensuring a complete experience for everyone.

One of the highlights of Neretva rafting is the opportunity to see the iconic Ottoman-era Konjic bridge from a unique perspective. The bridge, an architectural masterpiece, is a testament to the rich history and cultural heritage of Bosnia and Herzegovina. As you navigate the river, seeing this historic structure adds cultural significance to your adrenaline-pumping trip.

The trip also takes you through lush canyons and dramatic gorges, offering a sense of calm amid thrilling rapids. The Neretva River is not only a playground for adventure lovers; it is also a nature reserve with an opportunity to see various flora and fauna along the river.

After a refreshing day on the water, relax with a traditional Bosnian meal at one of the riverside restaurants and sample local delicacies that showcase the region and its culinary richness. This cultural immersion extends the experience beyond the rapids, allowing you to learn about local traditions and hospitality.

Rafting on the Neretva River is not only a physical journey, but a sensory exploration of Bosnia and Herzegovina and its natural wonders. The combination of adrenaline, natural beauty and cultural encounters make this outstanding activity in the heart of the Balkans, leaving indelible memories for those who dare to undertake this extraordinary adventure.

Skiing in the Bosnian Mountains

One of the most enchanting ski destinations in Bosnia and Herzegovina is Mount Jahorina, which received international recognition during the 1984 Winter Olympics. Jahorina is just a short drive from the capital Sarajevo and offers a diverse selection of ski slopes for all skill levels. Set against a backdrop of snow-capped peaks, this resort offers a versatile skiing experience, from gentle tree-lined trails for beginners to challenging trails for more experienced skiers. Visitors to Jahorina can enjoy not only the thrill of skiing, but also the warmth of Bosnian hospitality.

The area has a mix of modern resorts and comfortable mountain lodges where travelers can relax after a day on the slopes. The après-ski scene is lively, traditional Bosnian cuisine and lively local entertainment add a cultural flavor to the experience. Bjelašnica is another destination worth noting for those looking for a more intimate and remote skiing adventure. Known for its rugged beauty, this mountain offers a unique blend of challenging slopes and untouched wilderness. The crowds allow skiers to enjoy the tranquility of Bosnia's backyard, making it the perfect choice for those looking for a more secluded and authentic alpine experience.

In addition to exceptional skiing opportunities, the ski resorts of Bosnia and Herzegovina pride themselves on their affordability compared to many of their Western European counterparts. Reasonable prices for lift tickets, equipment rental and accommodation make it an attractive destination for budget travelers without compromising on the quality of the skiing experience.

Exploring Bosnia's mountains extends beyond the slopes, as the region is rich in cultural and historical significance. Sarajevo, with its fascinating mix of Ottoman, Austro-Hungarian and Yugoslav influences, provides a fascinating backdrop both before and after skiing. Tourists can immerse themselves in the city and its vibrant street life, taste traditional Bosnian delicacies and embrace the resilient spirit of a city that has overcome its war-torn past. skiing in the mountains of Bosnia offers an exciting mix of adventure, culture and affordability. Whether you are an experienced skier or a first-time skier, the ski resorts of Bosnia and Herzegovina offer an unforgettable experience amidst the untouched beauty of the Balkans.

Cycling Adventures

One of the most prominent cycling routes in Bosnia and Herzegovina is the Via Dinarica, a long-distance road that runs through the Dinaric Alps, offering cyclists a mesmerizing ride through some of the region's most stunning natural landscapes. The route offers the perfect mix of challenging climbs and exciting descents, rewarding riders with panoramic views of untouched forests, crystal clear lakes and quaint traditional villages.

For those looking for a more leisurely ride, the Bosnian countryside is full of charming cycle paths that wind through the picturesque landscape. For example, the Una River offers peaceful cycling that allows riders to pedal along the emerald waters and admire the beauty of the surrounding forests. With its cascading waterfalls and diverse flora and fauna, Una National Park provides an enchanting backdrop for an unforgettable cycling experience. Cyclists who like history and culture will find the city of Mostar an exciting destination. Known for the iconic Stari Most Bridge, Mostarand; cobbled streets and Ottoman architecture create a unique atmosphere to explore. Cycling through the city allows riders to enjoy the rich cultural heritage and stop at local cafes to try Bosnian coffee and traditional delicacies. Bosnia and

Herzegovina's cycling community is vibrant and welcoming, with many cycling events organized throughout the year. These events not only give cyclists a chance to show off their skills, but also foster a sense of camaraderie among participants.

The Sarajevo Grand Prix, for example, attracts cyclists from around the world to compete in a challenging race that winds through the historic streets of the capital. When planning a cycling adventure in Bosnia and Herzegovina, you need to consider the various landscapes and weather conditions. The summer months are warm and dry, perfect for mountain biking and trail exploring. On the other hand, the autumn season paints the landscape with countless colors and creates a landscape background for bike lovers.

To enhance the cycling experience, local tour operators and bicycle rental companies cater to the needs of travelers by providing well-maintained equipment and experienced guides. These guides not only ensure a safe journey, but also share knowledge of the history and culture of the areas being explored, adding depth to the overall adventure. Cycling adventures in Bosnia and Herzegovina offer the perfect mix of natural beauty, cultural richness and physical challenge. Whether navigating the mountain roads of the

Via Dinarica or leisurely cruising the historic streets of Mostar, each cycling experience reveals a different side of this hidden gem in the heart of the Balkans.

So, get in the saddle, breathe in the fresh mountain air and go on a cycling trip that promises equal parts excitement and peace.

Entertainment and Nightlife

Live Music Venues

Jazz Club Monument: Located in the heart of Sarajevo, this jazz club is famous among both locals and tourists. The club features international jazz bands as well as local performers.

Dom Mladih: is a prominent live music venue that hosts a range of genres, including rock, pop, and traditional Bosnian music. Other cultural activities held at the facility include film screenings and theater shows.

Kino Bosna: This one-of-a-kind facility, built in a historic cinema, presents live music events on Mondays. The venue is well-known for its varied vibe and emphasis on traditional Bosnian music.

Pink Houdini: A jazz and blues club in a more intimate environment, Pink Houdini is a terrific place to hear live music. The club features a range of local and foreign artists, and the drinks are reasonably priced.

Silver & Smoke Club: This underground club is popular among fans of electronic music. The club features a wide range of DJs and live performers, and the atmosphere is usually electrifying.

Monnet Café Bar: Located on the banks of the Vrbas River, this café bar is a famous venue for live blues and jazz music. The café bar offers a laid-back vibe and is a nice spot to unwind while listening to music.

Mala Stanica: Located in the city center, this restaurant features traditional Bosnian music every weekend. The restaurant has a rustic atmosphere and is an excellent place to learn about local culture.

Kriva Cirkva: This one-of-a-kind facility, built in a former church, is a popular destination for live music and cultural activities. The facility features a wide range of musical styles, including rock, pop, and traditional Bosnian music.

Bacchus Jazz Club: Located in the middle of Mostar, this jazz club is an excellent place to hear live music. The club features a wide range of local and international acts, and the atmosphere is always warm and inviting.

Cafe Kamerlengo: Located in Mostar's Old Town, this café is an excellent place to enjoy a drink while listening to traditional Bosnian music. The café boasts a lovely outside terrace with panoramic views of the city.

These are only a few of Bosnia and Herzegovina's many live music venues. With so many amazing alternatives, you're sure to find the right venue to enjoy some live music while learning about the local culture.

Nightclubs and Bar

- Club Tropics is located at elimira Vidovia - Kelija 121, Sarajevo, Bosnia & Herzegovina 71000. On Google Maps, it has a rating of 4.8 stars.
- Jazz Club Monument is located in Strossmayerova 3, Sarajevo, Bosnia & Herzegovina 71000. On Google Maps, it has a rating of 4.6 stars.
- Silver & Smoke Club is located at Zelenih beretki 12, Sarajevo, Bosnia and Herzegovina 71000. On Google Maps, it has a rating of 4.2 stars.
- Bambuss Club is located at S.H, ulaz, Muvekita 10, Sarajevo, Bosnia & Herzegovina 71000. On Google Maps, it has a rating of 4.6 stars.
- Trezor - Located at Kranjčevićeva bb, Sarajevo 71000, Bosnia and Herzegovina. On Google Maps, it has a rating of 4.2 stars.

Ribica: This popular club in Sarajevo's heart is noted for its amazing music and atmosphere.

Underground Club: One of Sarajevo's most popular underground clubs, recognized for its varied spectrum of music.

Kaskade: This popular club on the Neretva River's banks is noted for its gorgeous views and amazing music.

IQ Club: This sophisticated club is one of Mostar's most popular, including a VIP room and bottle service.

Club Infinity: This little club is ideal for dancing the night away.

Bierstube 90: Relax and have a beer with friends at this German-style tavern.

Staying Safe and Healthy

Safety Tips

1. **Embrace local wisdom**: Connect with the locals as you explore the beautiful landscapes and rich history of Bosnia and Herzegovina. They have valuable knowledge of the area and can provide information on safe travel routes and hidden gems.

2. **Stay informed**: Stay up to date with local news and weather. The diverse landscape of Bosnia and Herzegovina can lead to sudden changes in weather, so staying informed will help you plan your activities safely.

3. **Respect cultural norms**: Immerse yourself in the local culture by understanding and respecting customs and traditions. This not only improves your travel experience, but also ensures easy navigation in social situations.

4. **Beware of land mines**: Unfortunately, some peripheral areas still have remnants of past conflicts. Stay on heavily traveled roads and marked trails, especially in the countryside. Contact local authorities or your accommodation for instructions on safe routes.

5. Insure your property: Petty theft can occur in crowded areas or tourist destinations. Be careful with your belongings, use anti-theft bags and keep an eye on your valuables. Consider leaving important documents in a safe place, such as a hotel safe.

6. Transport security: If you plan to drive, familiarize yourself with local traffic regulations and road conditions. Public transport is generally safe, but be careful during rush hour and watch your property.

7. Health protection measures: Make sure your vaccinations are up to date and that you have the necessary medications. Bosnia and Herzegovina have a reliable healthcare system, but travel insurance offers additional protection in case of unexpected medical situations.

8. Emergency contact information: Save the local emergency numbers and contact information for your country and the embassy in Sarajevo. In unexpected circumstances, having this information readily available can be a lifesaver.

9. Wonders of nature: Whether you are hiking in the Dinaric Alps or exploring national parks, always prioritize safety in nature. Let someone know your plans, carry enough water and snacks, and be aware of the wildlife in the area. 10. **Connect with other travelers**: Joining local tours or connecting with other travelers will increase your safety, especially if you're exploring less touristy areas. Strength in numbers and shared experiences can enhance your journey. Remember that while these tips are meant to ensure a safe adventure, the heart of Bosnia and Herzegovina is its warm hospitality and breathtaking scenery. When you approach your travels with respect and a sense of adventure, you create memories that will last a lifetime.

Health Precautions

Here are some pragmatic health precautions to consider:

Vaccinations: Before traveling, check with your healthcare provider to make sure routine vaccinations are up to date. Also, depending on your travel plans, ask about recommended vaccines, such as jaundice A and B and distemper.

Travel Insurance: Get comprehensive travel insurance that covers medical expenses and emergencies. Make sure your insurance covers the activity you plan to participate in, such as hiking or water sports.

Water and food security: While tap water is generally safe in cities, bottled water is recommended, especially in rural areas. Be careful about eating raw or undercooked food and choose well-prepared meals from reputable restaurants.

Protection from insects: Bosnia and Herzegovina is known for its green landscapes, so be prepared for encounters with insects. Use insect repellent, wear long sleeves and consider accommodation with screens on windows to minimize exposure.

Sun protection: The sun can shine brightly, especially in summer. Pack and wear sunscreen, sunglasses and a hat to protect yourself from harmful UV rays, especially if you plan to explore sights like the spectacular Kravice Falls.

Medical devices: Find out where the medical facilities are in the places you plan to visit. Keep a first aid kit and be aware of emergency numbers, including local 911.

Tick Awareness: If you plan to explore the beautiful forests of Bosnia and Herzegovina, be aware of ticks that can spread disease. Wear long clothing and consider tick repellent, especially if you're hiking or camping.

Cultural Considerations: Respect local practices, including traditional health and hygiene practices. For example, it is customary to take off your shoes when entering someone's home.

Emergency Preparedness: Be prepared for unexpected situations. Carry a copy of your important documents, keep a list of emergency contacts and tell someone you trust about your travel plan.

Remember that while these precautions will help you have a safer trip, it's important to remain open to the unexpected and embrace the enriching experiences that Bosnia and Herzegovina has to offer. Take care of your well-being and let the vibrant culture and landscapes leave an indelible mark on souvenirs.

Emergency Information

If there is an emergency, please call 112 for immediate help. In Bosnia and Herzegovina, this is the universal emergency number that links you to the police, medical, and fire services. Always make sure that you have your mobile phone charged and within reach at all times. The healthcare facilities in Bosnia and Herzegovina are usually top-notch, particularly in larger cities such as Sarajevo and Mostar. It is recommended to have travel insurance that includes coverage for medical emergencies. If you need medical help, go to the closest hospital or reach out to your insurance provider for assistance.

If you have any safety concerns or need police assistance for an incident, please contact your local police station. They are usually friendly and easy to approach. Keep calm and try to speak in English when dealing with the police. Please make a note of the closest police station to your accommodation for easy reference. Knowing the whereabouts and contact information of your country's embassy or consulate in Bosnia and Herzegovina is a prudent idea. They are able to assist with lost passports, legal issues, and other consulate-related matters. Make sure to store a duplicate of your passport and important documents in a safe and secure place. Although

Bosnia and Herzegovina does not often experience major natural disasters, it is important to remain vigilant and aware of your environment. In the unlikely scenario of earthquakes or floods, please adhere to local instructions and move to higher ground if needed. Keep yourself updated by following local news sources or checking with your accommodation. Get to know the fundamental cultural norms and follow the rules and regulations of the local community.

For example, smoking is not allowed in enclosed public areas, and littering can lead to being fined. If you're wandering through the delightful streets of Sarajevo or heading out into the scenic countryside, make sure transportation safety is your top priority. Make sure to adhere to traffic regulations, opt for reliable transport services, and always fasten your seatbelt. When driving, exercise caution on mountain roads, particularly during bad weather conditions. Though English is commonly spoken, particularly in touristy areas, it can be beneficial to pick up a few essential Bosnian phrases. Translation apps are valuable resources for overcoming language barriers.

Local Healthcare Facilities

Knowing the local healthcare facilities is necessary for a safe and enjoyable trip. The country offers a blend of modern medical facilities and traditional healing methods, giving travelers a one-of-a-kind healthcare experience. The healthcare system in Bosnia and Herzegovina is well-established, with hospitals and medical centers located in major cities and towns. Sarajevo, the capital, has numerous esteemed facilities, including the University Clinical Center of Sarajevo, which provides a variety of medical services from emergency care to specialized treatments. If an emergency occurs, the country's emergency response system is dependable.

If you dial 122, you will be connected to emergency services with English-speaking operators ready to assist you. Ambulance services have the capabilities to manage a range of medical scenarios and to transport patients to the closest medical facility. The local pharmacies, or "apoteka," are widely available and easy to reach. They provide a variety of both over-the-counter and prescription medications. Pharmacists are typically highly educated and can offer guidance on common health concerns. It's a good idea to check the pharmacy hours ahead of time when in smaller towns. Traditional healing methods have been practiced in Bosnia and Herzegovina for centuries. Many visitors frequently seek out alternative therapies such as herbal remedies and thermal spas. Ilidža is a town renowned for its thermal springs, providing a one-of-a-kind healing experience.

Many residents swear by the natural elements' therapeutic benefits. It is highly recommended for travelers to have thorough travel insurance that includes medical emergency coverage. Despite the generally lower cost of healthcare in Bosnia and Herzegovina compared to Western countries, having insurance provides a sense of security and makes the process of seeking medical attention much easier. Even though English is common in cities and popular tourist spots, it's a good idea to have a simple medical phrasebook or translation app with you.

This could be especially useful in remote regions where English fluency may be low. In Bosnia and Herzegovina, travelers can access a wide variety of medical services, thanks to a combination of modern healthcare facilities and traditional healing practices. Visitors can have a worry-free journey through this culturally rich and historically significant destination by understanding the local healthcare system and taking necessary precautions.

Get your FREE book

Please visit https://tinyurl.com/travel-with-jeffery for additional resources and to engage with my newsletter.

I also want to reward you for purchasing my book. To get the reward which is a travel planner; kindly click on this link below or open the link on your browser.

https://tinyurl.com/travel-with-jeffery

I hope you love the travel planner!

Cultural Etiquette

Understanding and respecting local cultural etiquette will surely enhance your travel experience as you embark on your adventure through this captivating country.

1. Politeness and greetings:

Bosnians are proud of their hospitality, and welcomes are an important part of social relations. A firm handshake, steady eye contact, and a genuine grin are all regarded courteous and respectable. Until a closer relationship is established, it is traditional to address persons using their titles and last names.

2. Religious Sensitivity:

Bosnia and Herzegovina are home to a diverse range of religious beliefs, the most prevalent of which are Islam, Orthodox Christianity, and Catholicism. Respect for different religious practices is essential. To demonstrate regard, dress modestly, remove your shoes, and maintain a peaceful demeanor when entering sacred buildings.

3. Social Invites:

If you are fortunate enough to be invited to someone's home, consider it a privilege. As a mark of thanks, it is usual to bring a little gift, such as flowers or candy. Wait to be seated and convey your appreciation for the courtesy extended.

4. Dining etiquette:

Bosnian cuisine is delicious, and eating together is a social experience. Wait for the host to begin the dinner before expressing your delight of the dish. It's polite to sample a little bit of everything presented, demonstrating your appreciation for the time and work put into the preparation.

5. Language Considerations:

While many Bosnians understand English, knowing a few Bosnian words, such as greetings and thank-you, is always useful. Locals will most likely appreciate your efforts to converse in their language.

6. Personal Space and Gestures:

Bosnians are generally friendly and expressive communicators. It's normal to have enthusiastic chats and make welcoming gestures. However, personal space must be respected. Be aware of the level of comfort of individuals around you and alter your interactions accordingly.

Useful Resources

Helpful Apps

In this day and age, there are numerous helpful apps that can improve your travel experience, making it smoother and more pleasurable.

Maps.me

When it comes to navigating, Maps.me is a dependable buddy. This program, which includes offline maps, ensures that you won't get lost in Bosnia and Herzegovina's lovely but occasionally inaccessible regions. Maps.me delivers detailed maps without the need for a continual internet connection, whether you're wandering through Sarajevo's old streets or trekking in the Dinaric Alps.

TripAdvisor

TripAdvisor is a great app for discovering the greatest local experiences and hidden gems. You can locate the best restaurants, sights, and lodgings based on reviews from other tourists and residents. Bosnia and Herzegovina has a rich cultural tapestry, and TripAdvisor can help you navigate it to locate hidden gems that aren't in the guidebooks.

Google Translate

While English is frequently spoken, a translation program such as Google Translate can be extremely useful, especially when visiting smaller towns and villages. It bridges language gaps and allows you to communicate more successfully with locals, boosting your cultural immersion.

Culture Trip

The Culture Trip app is an excellent resource for learning more about Bosnia and Herzegovina's culture, traditions, and history. It curates' articles about local art, events, and historical sites to help you get the most out of your cultural excursion.

Moovit

Using public transit in unfamiliar cities can be difficult. Moovit makes this procedure easier by providing real-time transit information and route planning. From buses to trams, Moovit gets you to your destination quickly and easily, making your trips throughout Bosnia and Herzegovina a breeze.

The XE Currency

The XE Currency app is essential for staying on top of your finances. It gives accurate and up-to-date currency exchange rates, allowing you to make informed decisions when buying, dining, or planning your trip.

AccuWeather

Bosnia and Herzegovina have a wide range of meteorological conditions, particularly in hilly areas. AccuWeather provides accurate forecasts, so that you are prepared for any weather changes during your adventure.

TravelSmart

Nobody wants to think about an emergency, yet it is critical to be prepared. TravelSmart provides contact information for local emergency services, hospitals, and embassies. It also gives travel warnings, which keep you up to date on any potential difficulties during your stay.

Including these applications in your travel toolkit will certainly improve your experience in Bosnia and Herzegovina. Remember, while technology can be a wonderful advantage, don't forget to put your phone down every now and then to take in the gorgeous scenery and interact with the kind and inviting folks.

Useful Websites

A thorough selection of important websites for your travel guide is provided below:

Bosnia and Herzegovina Tourism - The official tourism website provides a wealth of information on attractions, events, accommodations, and travel tips.

Booking.com - A popular platform for booking hotels, hostels, and guesthouses in Bosnia and Herzegovina, with a wide selection of possibilities.

Feel Bosnia - To make the most of your vacation, keep up to date with local events, festivals, and cultural activities.

BH Airlines - BH Airlines' main website provides information on flights to and from Bosnia and Herzegovina.

Sarajevo Food Guide - This guide will help you discover the gastronomic joys of Bosnia and Herzegovina by recommending restaurants, cafes, and traditional meals.

Visit Mostar - Learn about the historical and cultural richness of Mostar, including information on prominent locations such as the Stari Most (Old Bridge) and the Old Bazaar.

Bosnia-Herzegovina Nature - Discover Bosnia and Herzegovina's beautiful natural landscapes, national parks, and outdoor activities.

Sarajevo City Transport - Information on public transportation in Sarajevo, including buses and trams.

Balkan Insight - Stay up to date on regional news and get insider travel recommendations in the Balkans.

Bosnian Language Learning - A resource for learning basic Bosnian phrases in order to communicate more effectively with natives.

Remember to encourage readers to venture beyond the usual tourist traps, to embrace local customs, and to immerse themselves in Bosnia and Herzegovina's distinct culture.

Conclusion

The country's unique position at the crossroads of Eastern and Western civilizations is reflected in its diverse landscapes, which range from the picturesque alleyways of Sarajevo, where Ottoman and Austro-Hungarian influences coexist, to the countryside's pristine lakes and rolling hills. Each region has a unique narrative to talk about resilience, reconstruction, and the indomitable spirit of its people.

The cultural diversity of Bosnia and Herzegovina is reflected not only in its architecture but also in the rich tapestry of traditions, folklore, and cuisine. The friendliness and openness of the inhabitants, as well as their genuine desire to share their experiences, contribute to an immersive experience that goes beyond conventional tourism.

Nature lovers will find solace in the undisturbed splendor of national parks such as Una and Sutjeska, which have gushing waterfalls, lush woods, and diverse fauna. The crystal-clear waters of the Neretva River and the emerald hues of the Pliva Lakes offer a refreshing escape, making it a haven for outdoor enthusiasts seeking tranquility.

As you say goodbye to this land of contrasts, you'll take with you not only memories of stunning landscapes and historic landmarks, but a profound understanding of a nation that has won over hardships and proudly embraced its identity. Bosnia & Herzegovina, with its untold stories and warm embrace, welcomes you to be a part of its story, turning your visit into a meaningful chapter in the country's evolving story.

Made in the USA
Las Vegas, NV
11 April 2024